Lives Intertwined

Lives Intertwined

A NOVEL

Anna Picari

Cover design by Lynn Andreozzi
Edited by Nicole Frail/Nicole Frail Edits, LLC.

Print ISBN: 979-8-218-51452-5
Printed in the United States of America

Prologue

Kim

Matthew and I met when I was in graduate school finishing up my Master of Social Work at Temple University. I was walking through the courtyard near the Philly-famous Bell Tower on a glorious September day. The sky was light blue, and for a minute, I somehow managed to forget that I was in the middle of an enormous city. Just as I made a plan to head to Fairmount Park to enjoy one of the walking paths, I stumbled. I floundered a bit, nearly tripping on a ladder upon which a man stood working on the sound system for an upcoming speaking engagement. I looked up at the same time he looked down.

I was waiting for a justified chiding—"Hey, lady! Watch where you're going!"—but instead he descended the ladder, tilted his head, and looked at me the way a dog looks at his owner when it's trying to decipher their human's curious words. He was a slightly above average-looking guy with a more than decent height, but he examined me with the most beautiful green eyes.

I don't know where I found the guts, but I asked him if he wanted to get a cup of coffee.

"You have to tell me your name first" was his reply.

"Kim," I said, meeting his gaze. "What's yours?"

He smiled. And it was *magic*. "Matthew."

We made plans for later that afternoon and met at a local Starbucks. I learned that he was a newbie electrical engineer, an only child like me, and that he was from Newtown, Pennsylvania, a suburb of Philadelphia. He loved the Phillies and the Eagles as much as I did. He shared that his mom called him Mattie. I thought that nickname was cute but didn't want to promote any oedipal feelings so I'd be sure to stick with Matthew or Matt. I decided this as though I already knew we would see one another again. He was one of the most engaged human beings I'd ever spoken to.

By the time the baristas were closing up that night, I knew Matt was someone I wanted in my life. If not for a serious relationship, then absolutely as a friend. But I quickly decided that I shouldn't try to place him in the "friend" category. I admit to having had many one-nighters—sue me for using sex as stress relief—as well as three longish relation-ships, which ranged from four months to a year and a half. But I felt a real spark of connection with this handsome ladder-climber.

Apparently, he felt the same way. He asked if he could make me dinner the next night, and I almost laughed. This was a first for me. No one had ever made me dinner. It's an intimate gesture, right? Needless to say, I was very attracted to Matthew. He was self-assured and easy on the eye. So I said yes. He texted me his address, and I was relieved when he confirmed he didn't live with his parents.

I arrived at his apartment, which was in the heart of South Philly, promptly at seven, and Matthew opened the door holding a long spat-ula. He looked adorable in a vintage Doors T-shirt and jeans. I mean, he looked *amazing* in those pants. My mind raced to envision him out of them, but I quickly regrouped, scolding myself. Matthew offered me something to drink, and I asked if he had wine. He poured us both a glass.

"I hope you like hamburgers," he said as he handed me my glass.

"Oh, I'm vegan."

Matt's face turned beet red, but he exhaled loudly when I laughed and rushed to tell him that I actually loved burgers.

I remember three things from that night: 1) I was with a good man, a solid man; 2) the man could grill a burger; and 3) when I looked into his eyes right before our first kiss, I felt seen and understood. For

                                                            Anna Picari

example, when we chatted about our parents, Matthew immediately chimed in about the importance of family, which was a good thing because, being an only child, I was very tight with my mom and dad.

After that night, we were inseparable. I moved in with Matt five months later. A year later, we were engaged.

Our wedding was held at the Sacred Heart of Jesus Catholic Church. Although I no longer considered myself Catholic, this was important to Matthew's family and to my parents, who consider themselves *very* Catholic. The wedding was intimate, around fifty people. We only wanted people who we knew would be in our lives for the long haul. My closest friend, Kana, served as my matron of honor and Matt's best friend, Greg, served as best man.

After our honeymoon in Italy, we settled into the house we purchased: a fixer-upper. While painting or laying tiles, we would chat about how many children we wanted and what they would look like. One late afternoon after a full Saturday of painting, we lay down on the floor in our living room, looking at the freshly painted ceiling, our bodies parallel but our hands touching. I said, "So, Orsetti. This is our home."

"This is our home," Matt repeated as he squeezed my hand. "And there is no one I'd rather home with than you."

I rolled onto my side and admired my handsome husband, picturing family dinners and growing old together. Little did I know the universe had vastly different plans for us.

Part I

January–March

Julia

Entry 1

Hello, Mr. J. I am sorry that I didn't write out your whole last name. I should prob know how to spell it since you have been my advisor/ English teacher since September, but it has too many weird letters and vowels that don't seem to belong. I don't know why we have to do this now. Why didn't we have to do this at the beginning of the year? I hope that this journal thing is going to make me better at writing plus I want to get an A in this class so I guess I have to do this. I just wish that you would assign topics or something. I don't know what to write. So I'll start with the basics. My name is Julia Suzanne Orsetti. My dad's mom's name is Suzanne so Mom made it my middle name. But I don't really see her anymore. Mom says it's because she misses my dad too much. Oh yeah. My dad died on the day I was born. Also, I have a brother named Deven. You had him in 6th grade and he told me that you are cool so I think you're cool too. I am exactly 5 feet tall and 104 lbs. with dark hair and green eyes. I live with my brother, Mom who you probably know, and our dog OP. He is brown and fluffy and is happy all the time. I wish that he would sleep with me but he is always with Mom. Anyway, my life is BORING. Like I don't know what else I am going to write. I hope the boringness doesn't lower my grade because that is probs all that you are going to get! This is all for now.

Kim

Getting to work on this freezing-cold January day was going to be worse than usual because now I have to change my shoes and clean up dog poop.

Mornings are hectic on a regular day, but they are exponentially worse on days that involve Deven and Julia fighting about their shared bathroom. Deven spends too much time in the bathroom doing I don't want to know what, and Julia is at the age where she has to do and redo her hair.

Because of the trauma-based therapy I had after Matthew's death, I can usually keep myself in a constant Zen-like state. I practice transcendental meditation, and it takes a lot to get me rattled, but the kids are really going at it now, and all the yelling this morning is about to send me over the edge.

I kick off my shoes and run upstairs in my stockinged feet. "What the hell is happening here?"

"She keeps banging on the door," Deven bellows and pokes his head out of the bathroom.

"He has been there for a half hour," Julia counters, kicking the door hard in her UGG slippers, momentarily opening the door wider.

"This stops here," I say through gritted teeth. "Julia, use my bathroom. Dev, finish up. You both have about five minutes and then I am leaving without you!"

I turn and head back downstairs to finish cleaning up and search for another pair of shoes to wear. While rummaging through my closet, I see the running shoes Matthew was wearing when he died, and it knocks the wind out of me.

I manage to stand and take a deep breath before dropping again to the floor, picking up the pair of shoes, and hugging them, feeling Matthew in my grasp. I give myself a minute, kiss the top of both shoes, and put them back exactly where they were. With the help of my parents and Kana, I had managed to collect and donate much of Matthew's stuff. But I kept the sneakers for a reason that I could never discern in therapy or on my own.

As the sound of arguing rings out in the distance, I ponder my children. The complex workings of genetics stuns and somewhat confuses me. I guess I always imagined that any daughter I would have would resemble me. But no. Julia has Matthew's dark hair and beautiful green eyes. When I look into them, I am both comforted and heartbroken. But her personality—that's all me. Sensitive, nurturing, a little bit of a know-it-all but kind to everyone. Deven resembles me with a lighter skin tone, sandy blonde hair, and light brown eyes, but his height and his personality are all Matthew. He is charismatic and remembers everyone's name. He doesn't get stressed easily and is well liked by his peers and teachers.

One of the downfalls of working at my kids' school and doing what I do is that Deven and Julia are held to a higher standard than other students. I am a Licensed Clinical Social Worker (LCSW) at Freedom Charter School in Philadelphia (Go Warriors!). The school is a K–12 that encapsulates the best and brightest in North Philly. My principal, Dr. Amanda Perry (Mandy), reminds me often that my role is fluid. Sometimes, I'm a therapist to a student, and a few minutes later, I may be walking a new teacher off a metaphorical ledge. Often, I'm giving parenting advice to those who claim "We've tried everything." And once, I even cave-crawled under a stall in the girls' bathroom when a first grader refused to come out. She was crying, her face red and blotchy, and clutching a big, pink eraser in her hand. I had gummy bears in my pocket, so I opened the package and we snacked and chatted in the stall while I played detective, discovering that one of her classmates had told her that he didn't like her freckles and that she should erase them. So she'd locked herself in. I'd managed to calm her down and walk her to the clinic.

So, it stands to reason, that if my kids were hot messes, what faith would the faculty and parents have in my ability to help their children? Deven and Julia are not perfect, but they are presentable in public and generally good people. Not that the episode from this morning testifies to that fact.

As we walk through the front door of the school, Deven lingering behind, Mandy pops out and asks me to join her in her office. I sit in one of the overstuffed chairs and Mandy takes her spot behind her desk. I like Mandy a lot, both as an administrator and as a friend. So I recognize her "concerned face" as she asks me if I have seen Oliver McDaniel recently. Oliver, Deven's closest and longest friend, having met when they were much younger, is also a junior.

"No, I haven't met with him recently. Is something up?"

"He's failing chemistry, algebra II, and Spanish. If he doesn't pull these grades up to a C by the end of the quarter, he'll be suspended from the basketball team. I don't know if something is going on at home or at school."

I know Oliver well enough to know he lives for basketball. It gives him focus and an outlet for all of his teenage angst. He is a polite boy but holds his emotions close.

"I'll grab him today before his lunch. I'll shoot you an email after we come up with a plan," I say. I send myself a voice reminder and head to my office.

My office is toward the back of the school, close to the cafeteria and the gym for three reasons: all the drama happens in PE and in the cafeteria, it is located between the upper and lower schools, and it was the only space available when Mandy decided that the school needed a social worker. My space resembles a living room with a sectional couch and a coffee table in the middle. The students plop down on the sofa and toss their backpacks on the floor, just like they would at home. And just like at home, a mini fridge is in the corner of the room, stocked with water bottles, soda, yogurts, string cheese, and other assorted goodies that kids like.

My workspace is relegated to a small corner so that the sitting area is warmer and more welcoming. I grab my laptop out of my work bag, check my emails and respond to any dire ones, and then review my meetings and student observations for the day. I see an opening in the late morning and send an e-appointment slip to Oliver.

Deven

Mom may win the award for being the biggest pain in the ass. I know she means well, but she always wants to talk. She wants to talk about freaking everything. Her current topic of choice is sex. She asked me if I was sexually active. I just said, "Mom!" and she backed off that particular question, but then came new rapid-fire questions.

Yes. I know how to use a condom.

No. There is no one I am interested in.

Yes. I know that you will love me if I am gay. That last one cracks me up. If she knew what I was watching on PornHub, she would realize that she never, and I mean, *never* has to worry about me being gay.

I wish my dad was here. I lied to my mom. There's a girl that I know that I can't look at without getting a boner. Her name is Zory, and she is a fucking goddess. I hear that her mom is Nigerian and her dad is a white guy. Z is more than super-hot. She cares. She is in charge of the club that takes care of the community. You know, the club that collects food at Thanksgiving and presents at Christmas time. I'm not sure how she feels about me, but I sit close to her in two classes, pre-calc and Spanish. Alphabetically her last name, O'Dell, comes right before mine, Orsetti. The seating-chart gods have shined upon me. My plan is to ask her to hang out by the end of the school year. My best friend, Oliver, thinks I have a good shot. And he would tell me the truth.

Oliver moved to our street and then transferred to Freedom from some catholic school. I don't know. Our Lady of Pathetic Losers or some shit like that. Anyway, he somehow butted into our basketball game at PE his first day, and that was it. Oliver is quiet. I mean, he talks a lot when it's just the two of us, but basically, he is a shy guy. He likes to be in the background and keeps his head down at school. His personality changes a lot when he is on the basketball court, though. It's crazy to watch. He's a machine. It looks like he takes everything that he hasn't said during the day and brings it to the court. Fire, for sure.

Oliver is my brother from another mother. I love his parents, especially his dad. I am so jealous that he has a cool dad. I don't remember my dad. My grandfather, who we call Pops, tries to be like a dad, but he is old, like in his sixties or seventies. I don't even know. Old people all look alike. Oliver's dad wants me to call him by his first name, Shawn, but I call him Dr. McDaniel or Dr. McD. I don't know what kind of doctor he is, but I think he does surgeries, so he is probably important. His parents are divorced, but they live in the same house, which is weird. I don't know why. They just do. Oliver's mom (I don't really call her anything) sleeps in the big bedroom and is never home or is asleep.

Shawn sleeps in the pimped-out basement. Shawn's crib, as Oliver calls it, is really sweet. It has a seventy-inch television with every gaming system you can think of and a small kitchen filled with everything you don't want your kids eating—or drinking, for that matter. When Shawn isn't home, Oliver and I hang there. Sometimes we get into Dr. McD's stash of Yuengling cans and play *Fortnite* or *Super Smash Bros.* I think that Dr. McD knows we take his beer but doesn't care. I think he likes that Oliver and I are friends because Oliver doesn't seem to like to hang with anyone else.

Kim

As I contemplate my day, I find myself staring down at my shoes and recalling how I'd frantically changed them at the last minute after stepping on a pile of dog poop before leaving for work this morning. I remember uttering under my breath *"Fuck, Optimus Prime!"* and then I immediately feel like crap.

Just to clarify, Optimus Prime is not some weird, trendy profanity. It's the name of my thirteen-year-old Mini Goldendoodle who we usually call OP, which is pronounced like Opie. My old friend had cowered and put his tail between his legs, and I'd bent down immediately to comfort him. I credit OP (and a ton of therapy) with helping me through my grief. The dog was a sadness-ridden impulse buy, but I'd needed a distraction for both me and Deven, who had been four at the time. Deven had the honor of naming him after his favorite Transformer.

My ringing phone breaks me out of my perseverating. I grab the receiver and answer, "This is Kim."

Deven

In the middle of Spanish, Oliver got a notification that he had an appointment with Mom during our lunch period. I know this because he sits next to me at a workstation. I ask (not en Español), "What's up with that?" with a slight nod to the notification on his iPad.

"I dunno," Oliver says with a small shrug as he pretends to do his Spanish work.

I'm barely paying any attention to Oliver because Zory is right next to him. I glance over at Zory's iPad and say, "Gran trabajo. Eres bueno en esto."

"Tell that to my grades," Zory says with a little smirk, which totally brings every cell in my body to full attention, which leaves my brain nothing to say.

"Uh, that can't be true," I manage to stammer. And then the bell rings, signaling the end of the period.

While walking out with Oliver, I ask, "Weight training before practice?"

Oliver says, "Yeah," and looks weird, like he has something he wants to say.

"See you in the gym," I say over my shoulder as I head to my next class.

Kim

My morning was wild. I had to break up a verbal fight between two fourth-grade girls and then meet with them to remind them of our school kindness code and the universe's need for girls to be supportive of other girls. This was followed by back-to-back meetings with parents and a pile of reports that needed to be read, recognized, and filed. So, I'm startled when I see Oliver in my doorway at 11:40, but I quickly recover and invite him in.

"Hey, Ms. O," Oliver says politely.

I offer him a seat and ask him how he's been.

He weakly shrugs and stammers, "Fine, I guess."

I make a quick assessment of his demeanor and come to the realization that Oliver is not fine. He looks depressed. He appears smaller somehow. It's as though he's a ghost of himself, just passing through life.

"Is something going on? And please remember that what we talk about is private unless it's something that cannot be kept just between us. In that case, you and I will discuss what we talk about with your parents."

Oliver, who is staring at his hands in his lap, looks up briefly and utters, "I know."

I have known Oliver since he was around seven years old. Oliver's parents purchased a fixer-upper down the street from our house on North Orianna Street in the Northern Liberties section of Philadelphia. Northern Liberties was founded by everyone's favorite Quaker, William Penn, and the neighborhood has gone through many changes throughout the years.

I break from my momentary reminiscing and look at this sweet teenager before me. I still see the hyperactive little boy he once was. Oliver was a gift for Deven. They rode bikes together and eventually found the basketball courts at Nelson playground. They would play for hours. They still do. He holds a very special place in my heart because he is an unofficial part of our little family.

"What's going on, Ol?" I ask gently.

We sit in silence for what feels like an eternity, and then I watch a single tear slide down his left cheek. I grab the tissue box from the coffee table and bring it to him, using it as an excuse to sit closer. I know his parents, Shawn and Aubrey, but not well. I believe that they are divorced now, and I only see one or the other infrequently.

Looking at Oliver, I have a sudden urge to wrap him in a tight hug but restrain my nurturing impulse to do so. Instead, I put my hand on his arm and say, "If you don't want to tell me what's going on, at least tell me what you need. What can I do to help?"

For the first time, Oliver looks at me. "It's all good."

"Well," I say gently, "can I support you in trying to improve your grades?"

"I guess you know about that." Oliver wears the beginning of what appears to be a smile.

"Yeah," I say with a smile of my own. "I kind of know a lot of things. So let's start with this."

Oliver watches as I pull up his grades on my laptop. He looks embarrassed but I keep things factual and nonjudgmental. I know about his ADHD and the struggles that come with that diagnosis. I focus on his algebra grades, noting that he is missing several (and by several, I mean *a lot* of) assignments. "Do you think a math tutor would be helpful?"

"Nah. I had one before. And I get what's going on. I just hate homework," Oliver says.

Oliver and I review all his grades, and finally I say, "Okay, let's do daily check-ins. Every morning before the first bell, stop by and we'll go over everything due for that day. That way, we know what's outstanding and what's been completed. How does that sound?"

With a minor grunt of acquiescence, Oliver heads for the cafeteria. I stop him before he exits my office and say, "Ask Deven for help. I know he would be happy to help."

Oliver just nods and goes about his day. I feel good about our conversation and really believe we can turn Oliver's grades around. I shoot Mandy a quick email and then I put the meeting on my mental back burner and go about my workday.

Deven

Pre-calculus. My last and favorite class of the day because it contains my two favorite females: Zory and Ms. Everitt are the hottest student/teacher combination I have ever had. Everyone says that Ms. Everitt is like twenty-three and doesn't have a boyfriend. This is probably true based on information the girls get from the personal questions they're always asking her before and after class. I can hardly look at her because, well, you know.

The good thing is that I like math. It comes easy for me, and I don't have to study for tests. Mom says that my dad was a math whiz so I guess that's where my math brain comes from. We are learning about how to graph limaçon polar equations. I love this. Anytime I get to use the axis, I'm good. It's unfortunate news for Zory, though, who is not good at this. During co-op time, we get to partner together. She smells so good, like a vanilla-scented goddess. I focus harder on the problem because, well, you know. . . .

The bell rings, and we walk out together. "Nos vemos mañana en la clase de español," I say, flexing my Español muscles. Zory smiles and gives a wave as she turns in the direction of her locker.

I hurry to my own and grab my gym bag before continuing to the weight room, which is small and located next to the gym's locker rooms. After I get changed, I realize Oliver isn't there yet, so I text him. And then the ... appears.

Then it disappears.
Then it appears again.
Then it disappears.

r u coming?

can't.
Sorry.
I'll text you later.

I go about my workout and talk to some of the guys there. It's the end of basketball season, and we're heading to playoffs and tournaments. After about an hour and a half, I grab my shit and head to find my ride, which means going to the car and waiting for Mom to get Julia from after-school sessions. She goes to the math lab for extra math practice.

I have a key to her car because I got my license over winter break, so I decide to get in and start it. Pop promised me his car when his new set of wheels comes in, which should be any day. Learning to drive with my automobile-phobic mother was the most stressful thing ever. Mom is a neurotic driver and a major pain in the ass when I am behind the wheel. I know that my dad died in a tragic accident, but what are the odds that lightning will strike twice?

Julia

Entry 2

Hey, Mr. Jablanofsky . . . haha. I learned how to spell it. But if it's OK with you, I will keep calling you Mr. J. or something shorter. It will sound cooler and take less time to write. I asked my mom this morning how to spell your last name and she asked why I was asking. I told her I need it for an assignment for English and since she was crazy this morning she didn't grill me with a hundred questions. She just wrote your last name down on a post-it and handed it to me.

Anyway, am I supposed to be writing this to you? Or just write? You say that you want this to be a free-thinking assignment, but I am just going to write about my day. I woke up, had a fight with my brother about him taking too long in the bathroom and then ate breakfast. Well it wasn't really breakfast. I grabbed a Kind bar and ate on the way because my mom was being a psycho about us being late. My mom had a meeting or something this morning. I really hate that my mom works at my school. Please don't tell her that. But sometimes I think she cares more about the other students than she cares about me. How many sentences is this supposed to be? Bye for now.

Kim

My cell phone rings toward the end of the day. It's Kana. I swipe to answer. "Hey."

"Hey, Kimmie. Busy?"

I laugh. "For you? I am never busy." But I know what she wants.

"So?" she asks in a way that makes the word sound like *soooooooooo*.

"So what?" I respond flippantly because I don't want to discuss my latest disaster.

"Don't be rude. It doesn't look good on you," she says, sounding exasperated, which is exactly what I wanted.

Kana has been pressuring me, on and off, to go out for the last two to three years. And by "go out," I mean with men. She feels that it's been a long time coming and that I wrap myself up in work and my kids as a means of avoiding anything romantic. In the past couple of years, I have been on exactly three dates and am ready to call it quits. She knows about the first two dates, but I haven't given her deets on the latest date, which happened last Saturday night. I suggest we meet at our favorite coffee shop.

Thirty minutes later, I arrive to see Kana sitting in a quiet booth near the back. I slide into the booth across from her and shrug out of my jacket, letting it fall onto the seat under my butt. I slowly sip on the double nonfat latte she ordered for me, lift my view over the cup, and stare into her eyes, waiting for the barrage of questions.

Kana raises her right eyebrow, leans back, and crosses her arms.

I continue this standoff.

Finally, she says, "Come on, Kim! Tell me about the date!"

I put my cup down and prepare to share the latest in the trifecta of shitty dates.

I raise a finger and state: "There will be no questions until I finish sharing all the lovely details of my date with Vinnie." Vinnie is the man I met at the Whole Foods in Center City Philly.

Kana acquiesces and leans forward, her elbows on the table and her iced coffee in her hands.

So I begin. "Vinnie and I made arrangements to meet at Manny's Bar last Saturday night at six thirty. I got there on time and managed to find a small table to wait. And wait, I did. And then I got to wait some more. I did get a text at six fifty from him that said that he was running late and would be there soon. So, I called the server over and ordered a glass of chardonnay. He showed up at seven twenty. *Seven twenty*, Kana! Did you hear what I just said?"

Kana starts to respond, but I hold up a finger again and she closes her mouth.

"That was a rhetorical question," I say quickly.

Continuing, I say, "Vinnie sat down like he was right on time and started to make comments about the Sixers game that was on one of the six television screens over the bar. I stupidly decided to take the high road and ask how his dinner had turned out, since that's what he'd been shopping for when we met. Initially, the man looked at me, confused. And then a sheepish grin spread across his face, Kana. Turns out, Vinnie was at Whole Foods because pork ribs were on sale and he wanted to have them on hand for the Eagles game on Monday night. He then went on to share the process of making ribs in a smoker. And the regaling of that mind-numbing process took over half an hour.

"Kana, for your listening pleasure, I will share with you now the abridged version of how to make smoked ribs. First, you put hickory wood chips in the smoker and put your seasoned ribs in there for about five hours. Do you know what he seasoned the ribs with?"

I quickly hold up a finger before Kana can speak, and I notice that she inhales and then drops her shoulders a little.

"Vinnie seasons his ribs with every spice known to man. I kid you not. He must have named every spice available at our local grocery store. But that's not the worst of it. He graphically described rubbing 'his secret rub' on the ribs. And that is all I am going to say about that," I add, disgust clear on my face, I'm sure.

I go on to share that Vinnie ordered a basket of wings without asking me if I wanted anything as well as two beers. I had stupidly thought that he was attempting to be chivalrous by ordering a beer for me. But turns out, the second beer was his because apparently the service is slow most nights.

Kana laughs, tears in her eyes, as I add, "The two-beered man and I made basic small talk in between his commentary on the Sixers game. And around nine o'clock, he asked me if I wanted to 'get out of here.' Obviously, I questioned where we would go, and he had the audacity to say, 'Your place is fine. My roommate is home sick tonight.'

At first, I was too stunned to speak. Was he expecting sex? What the actual hell? After this realization, I just laughed, told him to lose my number, and walked out."

Several seconds pass before Kana has the nerve to raise her hand.

I laugh and nod. "What?"

She takes a deep breath and asks, rapid fire: "Are you sure you didn't do something offensive like use obnoxiously big words? I appreciate your vocabulary but not everyone does. Did you bother to wear makeup? Were you in sweatpants? Did you brush your teeth or have pieces of chicken wings stuck in there? Did you suffer a stroke and say that you're a Cowboys fan?"

I chuckle at the last question. Kana knows that a brain injury would be the only circumstance in which I would be a Dallas fan.

The topic of conversation moves quickly past my date and into her own work drama. We chat for about an hour, ending with my proclamation that I am officially done dating because three strikes and you're out and all.

The rest of the week proceeded without much drama, both at home and at school, except for Oliver not being able to play in the first round of the basketball playoffs tonight. He has been checking in with me but often tells me that he didn't do this project or study for that test. At today's check-in, I made him sit on the couch and I took the overstuffed chair across from where he was sitting. I wanted to sit next to him on the couch and put my arm around him, but at school, I am Ms. Orsetti, not Deven's mom.

"So, Oliver. I want to help. You know I do, but I cannot do your work for you. Please, please tell me what is going on."

He rests his head on the top of the soft sofa, and I have a clear view of his neck, which seems unbelievably long all of a sudden. The pronounced Adam's apple catches me by surprise. This neck is the neck of a man. How does this boy have a man's neck? He must be around five-foot-ten, but to me, he'll always be a kid. He looks like a very sad kid right now, and my heart breaks a little.

I snap out of my little daydream and lean forward in my chair. "So, what are we going to do?"

"I dunno," says Oliver, moving his head to normal position.

"I think it's time to involve your parents."

Oliver stands up so fast that I jump a little. "No. Please. No. My dad is always at work and my mom is really sick."

"Oh, my gosh, I didn't know about your mom. Is she okay?" I ask sincerely. I haven't seen Aubrey for a while, but I had no idea she was sick.

Oliver says that she's getting better but has to stay in bed for a while. I notice that he doesn't share any diagnoses with me.

"Please let me know if there is anything I can do," I say as I stand and face him.

He says, "Yes. There is something you can do: you can *not* call my parents. I'm working on my grades, I swear."

I agree not to contact his parents—yet. But I tell him that he has two weeks to get his stuff in order. Oliver breathes a sigh of relief and then leaves my office.

Kim

It's Friday, and I have always liked Fridays. I feel accomplished because the workweek ended, and I'm looking forward to tonight because we always go out for dinner (or get takeout in the event of a global pandemic or sheer exhaustion). We will grab food later since Deven has a basketball game at five tonight. I may invite Oliver, Shawn, and Aubrey, if she's up to it, to join us so I can gauge Oliver's mood and maybe assess how sick his mom is.

Julia loves our Friday routine, but she's giving me grief about having to watch to the game first. She says she's old enough to stay home alone now that she's in middle school, and I couldn't disagree more. Julia is naive and a tad immature. I'm not ready to grant permission for her to stay home. She begs, "I'll be fine. OP will be with me." I remind her that OP is hard of hearing with hip and vision problems, and she relents.

Deven will stay at school to get some things done for Spanish Club and then he's going to head to the game. The team has to be there an hour in advance, so it works out. I leave immediately after the final bell on Fridays, so Julia and I go home to get changed.

On the car ride home, Julia tells me about a new student in her class named Allie. I know who she is because I peruse the files of new students, often before they are green lit to attend. Allie's recommendation from her previous school was a little concerning, but I keep my mouth shut. It's hard at times, but I must maintain professional confidentiality. So I simply say, "Oh. Is she nice?"

"Yes," Julia says excitedly. "Mr. J put her at my table, which is so much better because I was the only girl before." Julia goes on sharing about how they hung out at lunch together and have three of the same classes then asks: "Can she come over this weekend? I have her phone number."

"I guess so," I reply.

"Tomorrow or Sunday?"

Honestly, it doesn't really matter which day, because it's not like I have anything planned for the weekend. I am trying to think of a way to stall and maybe change the subject, though. I don't want Allie Bennett in my home.

"Let's talk about it later," I suggest, and Julia nods.

I'm so happy to hear that Julia has finally made what looks like could be a friend—she's so quiet and anxious that I worry about her tremendously—but I am just not sure if Allie is a good fit, knowing what I know. As I mentioned before, it's tough to have information on all the students in the building.

Kim

We arrive at the gym and immediately head to the concession stand to grab hotdogs and a bag of Doritos. It's a pregame ritual that Julia and I started when Deven made the team freshman year. It's gross, I know, but it's become a weird, superstitious ritual at this point. The team always plays better if we eat dogs and 'ritos.

We then find a seat a few rows above the home team's bench and watch the boys warm up on the shiny basketball court. I immediately find Deven by searching for his shoes: LeBron 20 Nikes in Laser Orange. The boys on the team weirdly resemble one another in stance and height, and I don't see Oliver, so I look down at the courtside bench. There he is, sitting in his warm-up suit and staring at his teammates on the floor. The buzzer sounds, and both teams head to their benches.

The coaches huddle their teams as the scoreboard counts down from three minutes. "The Star-Spangled Banner" plays, and then the captains go to center court and shake hands. The game begins, and I find myself frequently glancing at Oliver. I know his dad is sitting on the top bleacher, resting his back against the gym wall. I had taken note of him earlier when Jules and I walked to our seats. For the first time in years, I wonder how I have never really paid him much attention before. Shawn is handsome and not in a buff athletic way. He is the perfect blend of business and nerd. After Shawn and Aubrey moved in, I could barely look at them when they took walks around the neighborhood. Frankly, for years, the thought of seeing happy couples was like a punch in the heart. I even stopped watching any show that featured couples. Basically, I watched the Food Network or old DVR'd episodes of *Dancing with the Stars*. When I returned to work, I would occasionally see Aubrey and Shawn (always separately) and give a wave and a smile. For the last several years, I have seen only Shawn. I should check on Aubrey. Maybe she actually *is* sick.

Our Warriors beat George Washington High School 78-63. On to the next round: regionals. Julia and I head to the car to wait for Deven when I get a text.

> *I'm riding with Oliver. See u there.*
> *His dad is coming too*

> *OK. Great game. See you*
> *at Mario's. xo*

Deven

The game was excellent. I had two assists and made two baskets. The team had it together. A sophomore named Jackson filled in for Oliver and did a good job as point guard. I think a part of me felt guilty for being proud of Jackson. Like I was being disloyal. But that changed when we huddled up at the first quarter, and Oliver took his good ol' time getting his ass off of the bench to join us. His piss-ass mood is bringing me down.

By the time we got to Mario's, he seemed better. We sit at a table for six with Mom and Shawn on one side, Julia at the head of the table playing on her phone, and me and Oliver on the other side of the table. I want to talk about the game, but Oliver isn't interested, and he's being a dick about it. Then by the time the pizza arrives, we're both looking at our phones.

Kim

When Julia sat at the head of the table, I almost stopped her; it didn't seem polite for some reason. I thought about it and chided my antiquated thinking. No one is the head of a family. A family is a continuous body. Needless to say, we have a circular table at our house so we can see one another. Matthew insisted it was the best choice and would often joke it was big enough to seat a family of six. I always rebutted that I only wanted to be a family of four. Now we're a family of three with seating for six. No one sits in the chair that Matt used. I never really made it a rule of any kind. The kids kind of just knew. Maybe my mom said something, or perhaps kids are just that intuitive.

The over-the-top happy server, whose nametag reveals that her name doesn't match her personality *at all*, is placing water in front of each of us and asks if we want anything else to drink. The kids order various Pepsi products and then I order an iced tea. Shawn says, "I'll have a Yuengling Lager if you have it."

"You got it," the perky server replies, and I decide to mentally rename her Super Perky Server instead of using her actual name: Sue. I briefly feel guilty about judging her name, but she's just so bubbly that I feel justified.

Before she leaves, I quickly utter, "May I change my order?"

Super Perky Server says, "Of course."

"I'll have Kettle One on the rocks with a twist please."

"Coming right up," and Super Perky Server walks away.

Shawn and Oliver are barely talking, except for showing one another their phone screens. Julia appears mesmerized by whatever she's doing on her phone.

"Hey, Jules. What are you doing over there?"

"Snapping with Allie," Julia replies cautiously. She always worries I will confiscate her phone and go through it, but I have an app to do that for me. It runs in the background, and I get text alerts when something appears nefarious. It no longer runs on Deven's phone. I trust that kid and respect his privacy.

"Okay but phone away when the pizza comes." Julia nods, and as she looks down again, I continue talking to the very straight part in her hair. "Jules, did you hear me?"

"Yes, Mom. I promise to put the phone away. Happy?"

I simply nod as the server appears.

She delivers our drinks, and we put in two orders of french fries, one order of mozzarella sticks, and two original pies. Mario's authentic pizza pies are the absolute best in Northern Liberties. They are hand tossed, brick-oven cooked, and topped with homemade sauce and imported mozzarella.

Shawn raises his beer toward me and says, "Here's to the Warriors." I hold my highball up and we clink. We make eye contact (which Kana states is required when clinking glasses), and a peculiar feeling goes through me as I take a long sip of my K1. Shawn starts to make small talk, which is something that has not happened in years. Our past conversations centered around the boys and basketball. But tonight, things seem even more . . . awkward. Shawn asks about my job, and I give half answers. I am very protective of my work and my students. I take confidentiality very seriously, so I turn the conversation toward him.

"How are things in the world of otolaryngology?" I ask, and Shawn laughs heartily. The kind of laugh that fills my heart—the kind of laugh that Matt had—and I feel the sharp pain of grief. Those pains come and go, a pointed realization that my dear Matt is no longer on Earth.

 Anna Picari

"Wow! Most people don't know how to pronounce that word."

I snap out of my grief-lapse, smile, and reply, "Most people need to up their MD specialty game."

Truthfully, I looked up that word when we first met and never had a need or opportunity to use it. At the time, I believe Shawn was finishing up his residency at Thomas Jefferson University Hospital in Otolaryngology, and I wanted to find out exactly what he was studying. (The word comes from the Greek words meaning ear, nose, windpipe, and science.) Shawn shares that business is good and his schedule is more regulated because he has seniority in his group. Before I know it, Shawn is signaling Super Perky Server for another beer.

He turns to me and asks, "Another K1 rocks?"

I nod. What the hell? I rationalize. Deven can drive the two miles home. What's the use of having a son who drives if he doesn't come in clutch for his tipsy parent?

Super Perky Server drops off our second round of drinks, and by that time the appetizers arrive. I let the kids take what they want and then grab a handful of fries and put them on my plate. Just as I reach for the fries, Shawn also makes a move for the fries. His hand grazes mine and an electric charge courses through my body. What the heck was that? I suddenly feel the urge to cross my legs. I quickly redirect myself by remembering I am halfway through my second drink and I have to eat something.

Shawn tells both heartwarming and funny stories about some of his patient encounters. "LEGOs should add a warning label that states, 'Keep all pieces out of body orifices,'" he half-seriously says. Listening to Shawn talk about his patients as well as his son makes me confident that he's a good guy.

The evening passes quickly as Shawn and I chat about how the Eagles are doing and other miscellaneous things. But the one thing that seems to be lingering in my mind is how Shawn might be feeling about Oliver being benched when there were scouts at tonight's game. I play a quick game of mental ping-pong about whether to ask but then decide against it because he doesn't bring it up. Soon enough we're two pizzas and two finished adult beverages (each) in, and it's time to go. I sense that Shawn wants to say something to me but is hesitant. I gather my two kids, say goodnight, and hand Deven the keys.

Once we're outside, I notice it's snowing. I contemplate taking the keys from my inexperienced driver versus driving under the influence. I don't feel drunk, but I am, for sure, buzzed. I let Deven drive. We get into the car, buckle up, and I ask Deven, "Are you okay to drive?"

"Jesus, Mom! It's basically around the corner, and it's hardly snowing," Deven confidently responds, and he starts the engine of my 2023 Toyota 4Runner and backs a little too quickly out of our parking space.

My nails are digging into the palms of my hands as I mentally say the Hail Mary on repeat. As Deven is making the right turn off of Cambridge Street onto North Orianna, the car fishtails toward the curb on North Orianna. The three of us just sit there, and I think about Matthew's accident, and I know that the kids are thinking about me thinking about the accident.

I quickly recoup and say, "Close one. You did a great job handling the car, Deven."

A small smile forms on Deven's face as he slowly backs the car up, straightens out, and drives the two blocks to our house. I am still shaky as I exit the car, but I won't let the kids see it. Driving is a challenge in any big city, and I refuse to allow my neurosis to give them vehophobia. This is the fear of driving an automobile. I specifically looked this up after Matthew's accident because I could not look at the car for months afterward.

Before turning in for the night, I knock on Deven's door and he grumbles a "come in."

I hold his beautiful face in my hands and kiss his forehead. "Goodnight, my sweet boy."

"Night, Mom. Love you."

"Talk to you tomorrow," I whisper as I close his bedroom door and go across the hall to Julia's room.

I hear Julia giggling from the hall. I knock once and then open the door. She ends the call she was on and jumps up from where she was

                                                        Anna Picari

sitting on the floor, her back leaning on the bed.

"What?" she asks, her tone unfamiliar to me. I know she's twelve with raging hormones that periodically bring nothing but delightfulness, but it's hard.

I quickly change whatever face I had on and say, "I wanted to say goodnight to you. Were you talking to Allie?"

"Yeah. She was showing me something."

"What was she showing you?" I ask in a fake, nonchalant voice.

"It's personal. You know you don't have to know everything,"

"I know that, Jules. I was just making conversation. Relax," I answer evenly while thinking that my response should have been something about how having a phone is a privilege and that I am trusting that she is being appropriate in texts and such. But instead, I say, "I'm heading to bed. Good night, Julia. I love you." But I feel uneasy because it's the first time Jules has ever been cagey with me.

"Goodnight, Mom. Please close the door," my daughter adds while making a show of opening her AirPod case, slowly putting the left pod in her ear, then the right.

I do as she asked but wait outside her room to listen for whether she calls Allie back. She does but obviously I can no longer hear Allie's end of the conversation and Julia has taken to whispering. I take a deep breath, call for OP, and I go into my bedroom.

Deven

I take a shower as soon as I get home. I know that it's not my dad's fault or anything, but I am a little afraid of driving. The sliding on the snow freaked me out but I couldn't let Mom see. I want her to think that I am a confident driver, which I am not. And I really don't want her to worry. My license is only a few months old, and I'm still not allowed to go on major highways. Most places I need to go don't require highway driving, but I want to be able to drive to the Jersey shore by the summer and that requires crossing the Ben Franklin Bridge, traveling on Route 42, and then getting on the Atlantic City Expressway, which is a dangerous highway. People drive like complete A-holes and must be in a big hurry to get to the casinos or the beach.

I wrap myself in a towel and head back to my room. My phone pings. I look down and there's a text from Zory.

Buen juego, Demonio

I hurry into my room with a smile that probably looks like Jim Carrey's character from *Dumb and Dumber* when he was trying to hit it off with Mary from the back of the limo. Zory used my name. My Spanish name. I know that it's weird, but Demonio is way hotter than Deven. All of us were required in freshman year to find a name that's somehow related to our given names. I looked up the Spanish word for "devil" because it sounds like Deven and chose Demonio. Zory's Spanish name is Bronceada. I don't know if that's because she's biracial or because she likes the color. I should ask her some time.

Gracias, Bronceada ☺ 🇲🇽

R u busy?

I could be taking the SAT and would stop to text with Zory.

No just got out of the shower.
What r u doing? Did you go out?

I hope not. I don't even want to hear that she went to get ice cream with her mom. I wanted her to text that she was just waiting with her phone in her hand until she thought I had time to talk. She responded right away.

finishing up a paper for APUSH

APUSH is the acronym for that elusive course that only fifty percent of students pass: AP United States History. There's so much information to learn, with the amount of writing and documents, it's no wonder that most students don't pass.

haven't even started. LOL.

This is a total lie. I finished it a few days ago. I have to keep up with my work because basketball is starting to be a full-time job.

so studious 😁
wanna Facetime?

Fuck yeah, but I need to get out of this towel.

I'll call in a minute

I shoot that text right away and find a pair of shorts, put on my Temple T-shirt, run my fingers through my wet hair, sit on my bed, and hit the Facetime call.

The squawky tone plays, the four-note introduction starts, and there's Zory. Every time I see her, I'm struck by how pretty she is.

"Hey, Deven." Zory greets me with a smile that shows her perfectly straight white teeth. I want to kiss her so bad it hurts.

"Hey, Zory. Sorry for the wet hair. I just got out of the shower."

"No worries. Did you hear about the drama between Milo and Trevor?"

Milo and Trevor are the first openly gay couple of our graduating class. They're both pretty fem but they're cool. Milo is on the basketball team, and Trevor comes to every game decked out in blue and gold. He's a riot.

"What?"

"They had a huge fight after the game. A bunch of kids met up at Chickie and Pete's, and Milo was talking to LeDrew Hanson and Trevor lost his mind. He started yelling. I didn't even know that Trevor was capable of yelling anything other than 'Let's Go!'" Zory shares in what seems to be a single breath.

"I hope those crazy kids work it out. I'll text Milo a little later." Or never if Zory wants to stay on the call until the end of time.

"Yeah. They are such a cute couple. But anyway, want to hear a song from a new album I just got at the Record Exchange?" Zory asks.

I just say okay, and she turns around on her bed to grab the album, leaving me with the perfect view of the perfect girl's perfect ass as she does so. She holds up the "I Hate Myself and I Want to Die" album and puts the song of the same name on her record stereo system that's on a built-in bookcase. She switches back to CALL mode so I can hear better. I've never heard this song before. I'm not much of a Nirvana

Anna Picari

fan; I'm more of a Weezer fan. All I can think as I'm listening is that the song makes me want to die.

When the song is over and we're back on Facetime, I say, "That is the saddest song I have ever heard." This is saying a lot because my mom stays in her room and plays sad songs on anniversary days.

"I know. But the hardest part is that we're just listeners. We're not able to cure his pain," Zory states, clearly sympathizing with Cobain. And then I feel like an asshole for thinking that the song made me want to die.

"I think that if someone wants to kill themself, they'll do it. Do you remember that senior who did it when we were freshman?"

Zory has a weird look on her face, like she has a mouthful of Sour Patch Kids.

"We had that assembly two weeks later. Mom and Dr. Perry talked about the warning signs and all." This has added nothing to this morose conversation that we're having and I should have just changed the subject.

"I do remember . . . and ever since, I try to look for signs in people. You never know," Zory says.

Damn, she is so nice. I couldn't name one of the warning signs now. I really should look them up.

I take this opportunity to turn this depressing conversation around. "Hey, want to hang out tomorrow or Sunday?"

She smiles. "Sure. I can do tomorrow after seven. We're visiting my grandparents tomorrow afternoon."

When was the last time I saw my grandparents? Or even called them? I suck.

"Do you want me to pick you up? We can go to South Street."

"Sounds good. Good night, Demonio."

"See ya tomorrow, Bronceada."

And I finally exhale.

Julia

Entry 3

Hey, Mr. Jabla. That name is so fun to say. I am so happy that you told us on Friday that you would not be reading our entries but only would be checking to see if it's done. I feel like I can be more open this way. I know that you know there's a new girl in 6th grade. In case you forgot, her name is Allie. She seems really smart and is hilarious. I know that we are going to be friends. Her mom and her just moved to Philly from New Jersey because her parents just got divorced. Allie said that she is happy that they are divorced so that her mom won't cry all the time. I told Allie that Mom cries on certain days because my dad died the day I was born. Allie called it "tragic." I don't remember any of it so it doesn't really feel that bad to me. I get a little jealous and sad when my Pops has to take me to the Father-Daughter Dance but it's basically OK. I love my Pop. My Gram and my Pop are the best. They don't even seem like grandparents. Anyway, I think you'll be hearing a lot about me and Allie.

Kim

I settle in with OP lying on Matt's side of the bed. I wiggle closer to the dog as I think about Matthew, and I feel that void pierce my heart and my head. I remember lying exactly where I am now when my strong husband would wrap his arms around me. To this day, he is the only person I know who was actually able to fall asleep and stay asleep while spooning someone else. I smile at that memory. Most men simply roll away. And not that I blame them. I will never know how Matthew's arm didn't fall asleep. But maybe it did and he thought of my comfort over his. Ugh. That's probably it.

My phone chimes and it brings me back to the present. It's a text from Shawn. My heart does a weird thing as I open the text.

> *Just making sure you got home safely.*

> *We did. The roads were slippery.*
> *Thanks for asking.*

> *Glad to hear it.*
> *I had a nice time chatting with you.*

I was not sure how to respond so I went with the super original: "Me too."

*Would you like to grab a
drink tomorrow night*

I stare at my phone. Is Shawn asking me out? I have had exactly three dates in the last decade, and all of them were relatively recent. But before those, I had not one single date. Not a coffee date, no scratch-an-itch meetup, nothing. Nada. Zilch. I just had no desire to be with a man. Still don't. That's not saying that I didn't have a drawer full of sexual pleasure devices. I must have been in my head a little too long because Shawn texts:

No pressure.

I rub my temples and close my eyes. When I open them, I respond.

Sure.

*I'll come by tomorrow at 7 and we
can head to dinner. Do you like sushi?*

Only sociopaths don't like sushi 😁

You didn't answer the question 😊
See you tomorrow.

I immediately call Kana, give her the run down, and then repeat "What am I thinking?" over and over again.

"Would you shut up for a minute?!" Kana shouts me into silence. "Okay. What?"

Kana takes a pregnant pause. "You are thinking that you have not had sex in over twelve years and you need to make sure your vagina did not seal closed due to lack of use. And since none of your recent suitors did it for you, you believe that you are now and forever more asexual."

"I am such an idiot. Why did I say yes?" I mummer to myself more than to Kana.

"You are not an idiot. You are a very attractive forty-two-year-old," Kana answered.

"I hate the word *attractive*. It's borderline offensive. Like the word *agreeable*. It's boring and mediocre," I challenge.

"We need to go shopping tomorrow. I meant to say something to you before you started dating again, but here goes: Your clothes scream *social worker*."

"Oh my God. Do I have time to shop for something? My hair looks like shit. I'm going to cancel. This cannot happen until I have at least three months to get pampered and increase the intensity of my core exercises," I say, panic in my voice.

"Well," says Kana. "The nail salon opens at nine, and I'll see if my stylist can squeeze you in for a few highlights. No one can even see your abs because your oversized sweaters hide your entire torso. Now, go to bed. I love you. See you tomorrow at quarter to nine. I will have coffee in the car."

"Ugggggggh!" I respond and hang up. I conjure up a vision of myself, particularly my face. It's a good face, I think. I have naturally medium brown (a.k.a. mousy) hair with overdue highlights, and I am suddenly grateful that I'm going to the salon tomorrow. The best part of my face is my smile. I've been told that I have a great smile, and I agree. My teeth are fairly white and straight, thanks to Crest White Strips and the orthodontia that I had when I was fourteen. I'm only five-foot-four, but I work out daily and usually eat healthy, vodka not considered. I have to take care of my body because I'm the only parent Deven and Julia have. Not to sound morose, but I simply must stay alive for as long as I can.

Kim

I wake up at six, yawn my way into the kitchen, put a pod into the Keurig, and take my dragging ass and my coffee down the stairs to the basement.

I do a thirty-minute Hike class with my favorite instructor, Jess King, on my Peloton Tread. My basement is half laundry room and half Peloton showroom. I have the P trifecta: a bike, a tread, and a rower along with a big TV hooked up and connected to individual screens strategically placed in the middle of all three. That way, I can watch the very fit instructors sweat through the same workout I struggle with.

A little later, I take OP on a walk. It's freezing outside, and OP wears his light blue snowflake sweater. I'm careful to avoid Shawn's house for some inexplicable reason. I purposely walk in the opposite direction and come back the same way.

The kids are still asleep when we get back. Great. I take my time in the shower and shave my legs and armpits and assess my bikini area. It looks like the latest Chia Pet . . . Chia Vag. (New advertisement: Cha, Cha, Cha, Chia. Introducing our newest Chia Pet, Chia Vag. Hair grows on the Vag and down your inner left thigh.) I then debate if I should get a bikini wax. No! Absolutely not, because there will be no sex! I make a conscious decision to leave that area alone. I will not even contemplate sex with a messy bikini area. That settled, I get out of the shower and stand naked in front of the mirror.

I usually avoid looking at myself completely naked. I try not to get hung up on what my body looks like. I made this commitment to myself during one of the few minutes of lucidity while I was in grief hell. And the most absurd part of this commitment is that I know I should cut out the alcohol. I don't drink every day, but I know I drink more than I should. It just takes the edge off. I really wish weed were legal in Pennsylvania. Our neighbors in Jersey can legally smoke or pop a gummy. I'm too anxious to drive the measly fifteen minutes to go to a dispensary and then bring it home. I won't risk my state license or my job, so come on already, Pennsylvania!

I put on a pair of Lululemon pants and a soft long-sleeved tee. My hair is in a low pony, and I am putting on my Nikes as I hear Kana honking the horn. I grab my down vest and purse and head out the door, reminding myself to text the kids as soon as I get settled into her car.

Deven

I wake up with the biggest boner and stumble to the bathroom to handle it, literally. I hope to God that Julia is not in there. She's not. I lock the door and turn on the shower. No Porn Hub for me today. Today is all about Zory because she is the hottest person on the planet. I quickly feel guilty sexualizing her and remind myself that she is really kind, too. But I get over it quickly, and once in the shower, I think about her smile as I do my thing. It's over within seconds, and that is fine by me because I have to get going.

In the kitchen, I search for something to eat.

I see the text from Mom saying that she is out with Aunt Kana.

Great.

I go to the fridge and grab the OJ. I chug right from the bottle. I then grab a few slices of leftover pizza and throw them in the toaster oven. I eat them standing as I scroll through my phone.

I have a text from Oliver.

U awake?

yes. Sup?

It takes a minute for him to respond. That's happening a lot lately. It's like when I text with Gram. I think she has to have perfect sentences and punctuation because she was a high school literature teacher. But what's *his* problem?

Finally . . .

Can I come down?

Sure, man. use the front door code. in the kitchen.

Julia

Entry 4

OK, Mr. J. Can I just call you by your first name? I'll ask Kim to tell me what it is. You look like you have a basic name like Joe or Tom. Haha. Maybe I should start using her name when I write this because you know her first name like she knows yours. When I picked up my phone to ask about Allie, there was a text from her saying that she went out this morning with my Aunt Kana. I texted Good Morning but I forgot to ask your name. It is not important. Well it's probably important to you and your parents. What's important is that Allie and I are officially friends! I have to ask Mom if she can come over tonight, but it won't be a big problem because Mom is always around and if not, my lame brother may be home so I am covered for coverage. LOL I can't wait. I am going to see if we can walk to the Wawa around the corner and get hoagies and chips to eat for dinner. I love Wawa. I feel bad for people who have never been there. Bye for now.

Kim

Thank God that Kana brought me a large Wawa coffee, fixed precisely the way I like. She is a saint. We are heading to the Shops at Liberty Place in the heart of Center City Philadelphia. I will be able to get a mani-pedi and something stylish to wear, whatever that means. I usually get by with a decent pair of jeans and a plain shirt. I do have several pairs of boots, and thanks to a hefty payout from Matthew's accident as well as both life and mortgage insurance, I have a boot budget.

At Lyn's Nail Salon, Kana chooses black polish for hands and toes. I choose a nude color because I have no idea what I'm going to wear. My nails end up looking like they belong to an eighty-year-old, but what's done is done. Afterward, we headed over to Bloomingdale's Outlet. I find a gorgeous pale yellow cashmere sweater that will pair nicely with my jeans and low tan boots. Kana texted her stylist and got me in at 11:15. We walk the five minutes to Fifteenth Street where the salon is, and an hour and a half later, my hair looks significantly better. I offer to buy us lunch at the Reading Terminal Market and get sandwiches from Luhv Vegan Deli. I am not vegan but appreciate the movement. I choose a vegan option whenever it's available to make myself feel better on the occasions that I consume a Five Guys double burger. Why do cows have to emit greenhouse gasses? This loads me with guilt.

By the time we're back to the car, my watch says that my distance for the day is 7.2 miles.

Deven

Oliver comes into the house and finds me. He plops on the other side of the large sectional couch and yawns. I asked him if he slept okay. He said yeah. I don't believe him because he resembles a kid who was told that Santa isn't real at dinner the night before.

"Is something going on?" I ask.

He waits a beat and then tells me it's his mom. I know his mom a little, but she's never around. He tells me his mom and dad get into screaming matches because his mom drinks too much. I am totally floored by this information. I picture his dad screaming and it doesn't compute. Dr. McD always seems cool.

"She goes out to bars and then passes out as soon as she comes home. Sometimes she's not home when I get home from school. I don't know where she is. My dad doesn't know where she goes or when she'll be home. Honest, Dev, I think she uses drugs. I mean, I'm not sure, but she is practically asleep whenever I see her."

I don't know what to say, so I say the dumbest thing I could possibly say: "Ah, man. That really sucks."

"That's not all. My dad told me that the reason they still live together is so he can keep an eye on Mom. My grandparents are old and can't handle her." Oliver begins to cry. I move beside him on the sectional and wrap my arm around his shoulder. I don't want to say something stupid again, so I don't say anything.

Oliver stands and shakes out his arms and shoulders like he does when he's at the free throw line, then says, "Thanks, man. I needed to say that shit out loud." He grabs the remote control and puts the television on ESPN. We watch for a while and then Oliver whispers, "Thanks again, Dev."

I assure him that he can always count on me, no matter what. We hug and he turns to head out.

"One more thing," Oliver says, "don't say anything to your mom."

Kim

The second I walk into the house, I hear Julia bouncing down the steps like she used to when she was younger. "Hey, you!" I say and give her a side hug.

"Hi, Mom. Your hair looks amazing. When can I get highlights? Did you have fun? Let me see what you bought," Julia says in one breath as she grabs the shopping bag. She peeks into the Bloomingdale's bag and pulls out the sweater. "This is really pretty, Mom."

"Thanks, love."

"It's okay for Allie to come over tonight, right? You said she could come over," Jules states excitedly. I vaguely remember saying something about that.

"Honey, I have plans tonight," I respond gently. Boy, do I feel guilty.

"With who?" Julia demands in a sharp and surprised tone.

I feel resentful of how this question is delivered, as well as the tone used to deliver it, but I answer. "If you must know, I am going out with Shawn."

It takes a minute for this to register with Julia. With wide eyes, she asks, "Like Oliver's dad?" I nod, and then she follows up with: "Like on a date?"

I shrug and say that we're just hanging out as friends.

"Is this why you got your hair done? Oh my god. This is a date!

Aren't you too old?" Julia bellows. I can't tell if she's angry or upset or shocked.

"It's not a date, Julia! Shawn and I are certainly not too old. People that live in senior centers date!" I contend. "But if I was, it would not be any of your concern. And before you say something that will get you grounded, listen to what I'm going to say to you: If Deven will be home tonight, Allie can come over for a few hours. How does that sound?"

"Good. Thanks, Mom. I have to go find Deven. And the thing about the senior citizens is kinda gross."

She heads to the kitchen as I contemplate this new friendship of hers. Middle-schoolers change besties often, and I take solace in believing that this will fizzle out soon enough. But then a wave of sadness washes over me as I think of Jules without any close friends at all.

Deven

After Oliver leaves, I head to my room to dig through my hamper to see if I have anything that I can wash for later tonight. I am hyped. I pull out my favorite jeans and the light blue Tommy Bahama shirt that Aunt Kana got me for Christmas. Then I grab some underwear and a few sleep shorts and head down to the basement where the washer and dryer are. My foot touches the basement floor when I hear Julia.

"DEVEN!" she yells, sounding a lot like Mom. I hate living with two females sometimes.

"In the basement," I answer as I put my clothes in the washer. I hear her coming down the basement stairs, creak by creak. This house is over a hundred years old, and the basement stairs must be original, with a few new planks for safety.

"There you are," she says excitedly. "You'll be home tonight, right?"

"Why do you care?" I ask suspiciously. Julia does not give a shit about where I am ever.

"Because I invited my friend Allie over to hang out and Mom is not going to be home."

With the exception of going to my games or a meeting, Mom rarely goes out after dark. "Where is Mom going?"

"She's going out with Oliver's dad. Will you be home or not?" Julia presses.

I push past her, take the dilapidated stairs two at a time, and head to the kitchen.

Kim

As I am loading the dishwasher, which is full of dishes courtesy of my somewhat lazy children, Deven slides into the kitchen because he is running and wearing only socks on porcelain tile.

"Mom, are you going on a date with Dr. McD?" He is momentarily breathless from running up the basement stairs.

I'm startled by his abrupt delivery. I can't tell if he's happy excited or pissed-off excited. "It's not a date."

Deven looks at me dubiously. "Your hair is different. Are you trying to look good for Dr. McDaniel? Never mind. I don't want to know."

I am immediately defensive. "Oh, forgive me for actually doing something that is none of your business."

"It's my business when it's my best friend's dad," Deven responds in a voice that was about a four on a classroom voice-level chart. And deep down, I completely understand this reaction. I am invading his turf in some way.

I turn to look him square in the face. I tell him that Shawn and I are just going out for a drink, and we are just friends. I reiterate by repeating: "Just friends. I am not ready for anything more." That line was more for me than for Deven. I don't know what the hell I'm getting myself into. I'm not even sure what "anything more" even means.

"Well, you can't go anyway. Julia invited some rando over tonight and I'm going out with Zory."

"I assume you are talking about Zory O'Dell?" I state.

"Do you know any other human alive named Zory?" Devin asks flippantly.

I shake my head and let out a huge sigh. This is the first time in the history of this family that all three of us have something to do at the same time. I had a feeling that Deven had a crush on Zory for a while now and I don't want to disappoint him. Paradoxically, I feel a wave of loss. I wish Matthew were here so we would have another adult to monitor Julia and Allie. How fucked up is this? If my dead husband were alive, I would be able to go out with another guy without the extra BS.

My mind starts playing out different scenarios and then I offer, "I think it's time that I trust Julia alone with a friend." I see the relief on Deven's face. He hugs me tight and then heads upstairs. When he hugs me, I still smell his special brand of baby scent. It has not changed. I believe that I could identify both of my kids blindfolded by simply sniffing their necks. I wonder if all parents know their kids' scents. Deven smells like a hike through Fairmount Park—woodsy and smoky; Julia smells like cotton candy. I know that is bizarro, but she has always had a sweet scent. For a brief moment, I am sad because my kids are growing up faster than I am comfortable with.

Julia

Entry 5

Dear Mr. Jabba the Hutt. hahahaha. My family really likes Star Wars movies. I think I have seen them all. Anyway, you will not believe this! No one will be home tonight except for me and Allie. My mom and brother are both going out. This is the best thing that ever happened to me. I just texted Allie and told her and she is super excited. My mom is taking me to the store soon so I can load up on food. What's your favorite snack? Let me guess. You look like a fruit guy. I don't mean that in a mean way, but you always have those small orange things on your desk. I can't remember what they are called. I will let you know what we buy and all.

Kim

Since I am not comfortable with Julia and Allie walking alone to Wawa for snacks, I drive Julia to the store and let her go to town. My cart is loaded with so much sugar and fat that it's embarrassing, but Jules is so happy. The car ride home gives me time to reiterate my expectations. I make Julia repeat them.

"I am only allowed to use the microwave to cook. No one else can come over. I am to have my phone with me no matter where I am in the house and answer if you call or text. I should not open the door for anyone. I need to make sure that OP goes out to pee at least once. Allie and I are not allowed in your bedroom or Deven's bedroom. We can't watch any R-rated things on TV or on the computer. Did I forget anything?"

"Nope. Good job, Julia." I reach across the car console and grab her hand and give it a squeeze. I just hope that Julia is strong enough to redirect any of the behaviors that were noted on Allie's transfer packet. She had several referrals for being disrespectful to both staff and students as well as a suspension for smoking in the bathroom. I resolve to treat this new friend as though I don't have five years' worth of behavioral information sitting on my desk at work.

By the time I get home, it's almost six. Julia makes herself a Lean Cuisine in preparation for junk foodapalooza. Deven emerges from the bathroom in an old pair of Freedom PE shorts as I ascend the stairs.

"Hey, Dev," I say as I walk toward him. "Mmmm, you smell nice."

"It's just my deodorant. But thanks, Mom."

I think about what to say next because I don't want to be preachy, so I decide to tell him to have a great time, drive carefully, and remember that his curfew is at eleven. What I hold back is "Don't have sex without a condom."

He responds, "Thank you. Will do," to the former statement and walks into his room as I head to the bedroom to get ready.

Preparing for a date when you have not had a proper date (the three recent catastrophes aside) in over a decade is rough. I stand in front of the full-length mirror in the bathroom wearing my usual underwear, which is taupe. Real sexy. Matches my nails. *Tan, it's not just for grannies anymore.* And then I wonder why I feel compelled to wear nice underwear since I have no intention of letting Shawn see me in a bra and panties.

With a less critical eye, I examine my body once again. It occurs to me that it's easier not to body shame myself when no one can see what's under my clothes. I am confident about my body—it's strong and healthy—but I have to recognize the changes that have slowly happened due to aging. My once full and perky breasts sit lower on my chest, and my stomach has a pouch in the area under my belly button. Ugh. I admonish myself and change my attitude. I remind myself that my body is still in pretty good shape, and I am still attractive. My face has always fallen into the "cute" category, and I am grateful that, as I am aging, I remain in that group.

As I rummage through my underwear drawer, I stop and question myself. Why are my undergarments even a consideration for this date? I could wear any old bra with my Woxers. At the bottom of my drawer, I find a matching black set from Victoria's Secret, circa 2010, and decide that I would feel more sexual and thus, more in a "date" headspace, if I wear them. Then a realization pops into my head:

Oh my God.

What if he wants to have sex?

When Matt and I started dating, I was barely twenty-four. *Twenty-four.*

I am almost two decades older than that now. What the fuck am I doing?

I mentally reprimand myself again. *Stop the negative thoughts!*

I pull an old Phillies T-shirt from my bottom drawer, quickly wrench it over my head, and sit on my floor pillow. I meditate for about ten minutes and then finish getting dressed.

Deven

I yell goodbye to Mom and Julia as I put on my jacket and grab the keys to Pop's old car because his upgrade came in yesterday morning. I like driving, but it's hard to find parking at school since I'm not a senior.

Earlier today, Zory texted me her address and added, *See you around 7* with a yellow heart emoji. What the fuck does a yellow emoji mean? There should only be two colored heart emojis: red and black. Love and not-love. I immediately asked Siri. It responded that the "Yellow emoji conveys admiration and friendship." My heart actually plummeted. What if Zory sees me as a friend? I rationalize that it *was* a heart. She could have added any other freaking emoji . . . a smiling face, a cat, whatever, but she chose a heart. That's good enough for me.

Zory lives on South Third Street, and it takes less than twenty minutes to get there. When she texted me the address, I was a little surprised. Her address is in the Society Hill section of Philadelphia. It is in a historic area, and you can walk to Independence Hall. I would have bet that all the kids who live in her neighborhood go to private schools. Now I'm wondering why Zory doesn't go to a private school, but I won't ask her because that would be rude. And besides, not going private shows just how cool she is, like she knows that she's not better than anyone else.

As I drive down her street, parking's shit. I circle around twice, and then my phone rings. It's Zory. "Hey there. Is that you casing my neighborhood?"

"There's nowhere to park," I answer.

Zory laughs. "Sorry. I should have warned you. Just stop in front of my house and I'll jump in."

I tell her I'll see her in two minutes and make a left back toward North Third. Zory's house is in the middle of the street. It's clearly one of the originals and sits between some new homes. I spot her standing on the top step, waving as I slow down. My heart races and I feel my lower region coming to life. I breathe deep as she opens the passenger door and slides in.

"You look really nice, Zory," I say evenly. Mom has instilled in me to always notice when someone makes an effort. Not that Zory needs to try, but her hair looks different. It's down and curly and falls to her shoulders. Z usually has her hair in a pile on top of her head at school. And she's wearing lipstick. I try not to focus on that.

"Thank you. You look nice too."

I smile and head to South Street. I park in a garage because it's Saturday night. If you're from Philly, you know what that means. It's my favorite area of the city because it's loaded with eclectic stores and interesting people. And you can always find something good to eat.

"Want to go to the Tattooed Mom?"

"What's that?" Zory sounded skeptical.

"It's a food place. It's good." There are vegan options, and I want to seem considerate. I have no idea whether Zory is vegan. She looks like what I think a vegan usually looks like: she's one of those naturally cool people who wears very little makeup and clothes that look like they were purchased at a vintage or thrift store.

Zory slips her hand into mine and tells me to lead the way, and I pray that my hand is not sweaty.

Kim

Shawn is right on time. He rings the bell, and I yell goodbye to Julia and Allie. Allie had arrived early, but that was okay. She respectfully greeted me with a "Hey, Ms. Orsetti," and then the two of them headed up to Julia's room.

As we're walking out the front door, Shawn tells me that I look lovely, and my cheeks warm. Thank God it's dark outside in January; I feel ridiculous acting like a teenager. Shawn is handsome and confident, and right now, I'm anxious. I have a discomforting feeling this could morph into something more than friendship.

A fizzle snakes through my body, and I push down the memory of what is the beginning of a spark. As feelings and thoughts about Shawn flitter through my brain, thoughts of Matt wash over them like a tsunami. Small tears spring to my eyes as I think about how much I still miss him after all this time. I gently, and with some trepidation, push his image out of my mind and focus on the night ahead.

We walk to Shawn's Tesla, which is parked midway between our houses. I joke that I should have just walked to his house, and he laughs.

"I wanted to make sure the car was warm for you." He opens the door for me, and my butt sinks into the leathery, buttery, heated seat. I murmur a sigh of gratitude, and Shawn says, "Have you ever been to the Rosewood on Walnut Street?"

It's humiliating to think of all the places I have never been considering I was born and raised in Philly. Obviously, I have been to all the touristy places, but for almost two decades, I have been a homebody with the exception of when Kana drags me to Chickie and Pete's or somewhere just as exciting. My outing repertoire mainly involves something along the lines of Mario's, Chick-fil-A, or Panera Bread.

"No, but I have been wanting to try it," I respond. And it's the truth. Since the moment he spoke the name of the bar a minute ago, I have been wanting to go.

"Great. My buddy works there and will make sure we get a table. It's crazy there on Saturday night."

On the twenty-minute drive there, we talk about the fact that Shawn is from Chicago and went to University of Michigan but moved to Philly for medical school. He and Aubrey married before the move, and Oliver came soon after. Shawn alludes to the fact that by the time Oliver was in elementary school, Aubrey had changed. He doesn't elaborate, and I don't press. I quickly change the subject to the Eagles game tomorrow. I love my birds, and Shawn admits he's a closeted Bears fan. I jokingly tell him to stop the car, and he backpedals and adds the caveat that the birds rule over all—except when they're playing the Bears. I let him have that. I admire loyalty in sports fans.

We somehow manage to find street parking near the Rosewood.

Julia

Entry 6

Dear Mr. Jablanofsky. I am writing in the bathroom so I can get thoughts out of my brain and put them somewhere else. My mom could not get out of the house fast enough for me. She has to tell me 1,000,000 times that she loves me. Allie and I went right to my room, and she sat at my computer and asked me why I don't have a laptop. I didn't know what to answer because I never really wanted a laptop. She went on YouTube and turned on a music video. Then she asked me if there was any vodka or rum. I don't even know what rum is, but I know what vodka is because that is what my mom drinks. I told her that I didn't know, and she grabbed my hand and led me down to the first floor. She opened the freezer and pulled out my mom's bottle. I started to feel very nervous, and I told her that we probably shouldn't touch it. Allie told me not to be a baby and then opened the bottle and drank from it. I tried to look cool, but inside, I was dying. I know that I am going to get in trouble, and then my mom will never let me be home alone again. NEVER! Allie handed me the bottle, and I didn't know what to do. I took a little drink, and my mouth started burning. It was so gross. Allie held the bottle up so more poured into my mouth and I ended up spilling a lot. OP came and started licking the floor. I got paper towels and hurried to clean up the floor. I didn't think a dog should be drinking that. And then I said that I had to go to the bathroom. I am afraid of what else will happen.

Deven

After we eat, Zory and I hold hands and walk into some of the shops lining the streets.

"There's a vintage shop down here," she says, pulling me along. She could pull me to the gates of hell, and I would go. The store is really cool, and Zory finds a shirt and jacket that she likes and buys. I just rummage through the vinyl positioned around the perimeter of the store, and she comes and gets me when she is finished.

We head to Jaslin's and share a S'mores Galore. It seems so normal to be walking in the freezing cold weather sharing a spoon. Zory tells me that I look like a little boy eating ice cream and I smile, losing some of the marshmallow. She uses her napkin and wipes it off, and I feel all weird. But good weird.

Zory nonchalantly asks, "Is your friend Oliver a good guy?" and I stop walking, so she stops, too.

"That's a random question."

Zory looks sheepish and tells me there's a girl who likes him but she's protective of her friends and wants an honest answer to the question.

"Oliver is a good guy, but he's been a downer lately. I think his home life is crappy." What? She wanted honest.

"That's horrible. But I am more interested in the way he treats his girlfriends."

I tell her I'm not totally sure if Oliver has had any girlfriends, other than Paisely Morrow in fourth grade, and then add, "But he's a mild guy. I would think that he would be nice to anyone." This seems to appease her and we start walking again.

It's getting late, and I have about thirty minutes to get home, so we head to the car. I pull in front of her house and put the vehicle in park. She says she had a really nice time and leans over and kisses me on my mouth. I mean to pull her into a hug, but I guess she thinks I want to upgrade the kiss, so the next thing I know, we're French kissing.

Zory breaks away after a minute or two or a hundred and says goodnight.

I mumble something like "Goodnight" back and watch as she walks up her steps and turns, waves, and then closes the door behind her.

Deven

I get home just before eleven, and OP greets me at the door. Then I hear it. Julia's throwing up in the bathroom off of the kitchen. I hurry over and see the vodka bottle almost empty on the counter. I call, "Are you okay, Jules?"

Julia responds that she's *not* okay. I crouch down to where she's sitting on the floor next to a very messy toilet. "Mom's not home yet," she croaks.

My mind goes into DON'T UPSET MOM mode. I help lift Julia off the floor and get her to her room, where I tell her to get into pajamas and hand me her dirty clothes. She somehow manages to undress and throws her clothes into the hallway. I pick them up off the floor, and after enough time passes, I go in and watch her collapse face down on her bed. I turn her face to the side, because someone once told me that some old rock star died because he drowned in his own vomit.

I grab Julia's dirty clothes and some of the wet towels I left on the bathroom floor after my shower earlier and hurry back to the down-stairs bathroom. I use the wet towels to clean up any leftover puke and then put everything in the wash. Our washer is really quiet, and you can't hear it upstairs when the basement door is shut.

I then run back upstairs, add some water to the vodka bottle, and put it back in the freezer. I clean up the junk food trash and turn on the diffuser that Mom keeps in the bathroom.

My foot hits the top step as I hear the front door open.

Kim

I smooth my hair before I open the front door, my hand hitting the wrong code twice. I am still reeling from the make-out session that just occurred in the parking lot of a church, just a few streets away from my front door. The house is quiet, and I quickly take off my jacket and head up to check on Julia. She is fast asleep. I close her door and see that Deven's door is open.

"Hi, Dev."

"Hey, Mom. How was your date with Shawn? Will Oliver and I be real brothers soon?" Deven inquires sardonically.

"Don't be a jerk. However, the date was fun. We went to a bar on Walnut Street."

I sit on the edge of his bed. I ask him how it went with Zory, careful not to seem too interested. But in reality, I am very interested. Zory has a mysterious, yet very polite, air about her. Deven says the date was fun, and he feels like they walked for miles.

"Are you going to text her tonight?"

"Should I?" he asks incredulously.

I share that it would not hurt to thank her for being good company. He just nods and I reach over, hug him, and tell him that I love him more than anything.

He says "I love you" back, and I get up and close the door behind me.

* * *

As I head to my room, I am now secure in the knowledge that hanging out with Shawn was definitely a date. Shawn is a very interesting man with unusual interests. He is a third-degree black belt, which made me feel a lot safer walking with him through the streets of Philly, which is showing an alarming amount of crime. Shawn also plays the cello, which he swears this fact was the clincher for his admission team at the University of Michigan. The music department emailed him two days after the decisions went out and invited him to be a part of their orchestra. The most fascinating thing about him is that he speaks Spanish, French, and Italian. When I asked him if he travels much, he simply replied, "Not a lot anymore, but I hope to take Oliver to Europe after he graduates."

We held hands like teenagers on the way back to the car, and I felt a jolt of electricity coursing through my veins when he initially took mine in his. I told myself to calm down. Shawn chivalrously opened my car door before walking around to the driver's side. Not long after, at a red light, he turned to look my way and we just started kissing— mouth-to-mouth foreplay.

He smoothly pulled over near a local church, and we were practically on top of one another in the front seat. He kissed my neck, slowly moving up and down. I remember thinking this was what melting must feel like. My mouth found his neck, and afterward, I sucked on the tip of his tongue and slowly kissed his hungry mouth. He unzipped my jacket and slid his hands under my sweater. When he fondled my nipple over my sexy bra, I gasped, and a bolt of electricity shot straight down between my legs. I reached down and felt his erection through his jeans. I am certainly not a penis expert, but his felt thick and long.

And then I froze.

I thought about Matthew, yet again. More specifically, Matthew's penis, which is embedded in my memory. He had the perfect sized penis for me. We fit together as if the gods of love had manufactured us as puzzle pieces.

I mentally reprimanded myself for going down this rabbit hole, but needless to say, I cooled off shortly after. Shawn said, "I'm sorry if we're moving too fast."

I don't correct him.

He drove me home and climbed out of the car to walk me to the door. He gave me a chaste kiss and a strong hug and said goodnight.

* * *

By the time I close my bedroom door, my phone chimes. It's Shawn.

I had a great time tonight ☺

Me too 😁

But I wanted to add an eggplant and a taco. It's been a long time since my taco had an eggplant.

Are you free on Wednesday evening?
We can grab an early dinner

I had to go through my mental calendar. Next basketball game is Friday, Julia's dance classes are on Tuesday and Thursday. No meetings after school. Yep, I am free.

I am free on Wednesday.
I look forward to it.

Me too. See you on Wednesday
at 5:30, if that works.

Perfect. Goodnight. And thank
you for a lovely evening 🩶

Goodnight 🩶

I randomly picked a color that wasn't red because that seemed too intimate. I am not emotionally ready to send a man a red emoji. I have zero idea if the colored hearts represent anything specific, and the single reason that I know what the taco and the eggplant mean is because a ninth grader sent a text from his school iPad to an eighth grader with those emojis. I quickly open my Google app and look up the purple heart emoji and breathe a sigh of relief. I was panicking that it meant oral sex or something. It doesn't. It means several things, but fellatio is not one of them.

My phone chimes again. There is a text from Shawn.

Free tomorrow night?

That is an unexpected question. Of course my answer is yes, but I don't know what to do. Should I keep myself from appearing too eager? My brain is saying to say no, but my vagina is saying something different. Vag wins.

Sure.

Great. Dinner?

What in the name of God was that? Nothing says sexy like a thumb's-up emoji. I feel my face get hot just as Shawn texts back.

I will be by at 5:30 tomorrow.

And before I realize what I'm doing, I hit the thumb's-up emoji again. Jesus. I am a hot mess and apparently text like an eighty-year-old woman but at least my nail color choice corresponds.

I put on a pair of Woxers and a tee, happy to be out of the very wet thong that was riding up my ass. I lie in bed, overwhelmed with guilt and the need to orgasm. I put my hand between my legs and think about Matthew. He was so good with his mouth. I think about his mouth kissing between my legs, but images of Shawn doing the exact move keep overlapping. I orgasm and then orgasm again. I fall asleep almost immediately afterward.

Julia

Entry 7

Dear Mr. J., I didn't feel good when I woke up, and my phone was in the charger by my bed. And it says that it's 3:30 in the morning. It also said that Allie sent me a snap. I turned on my side and faced the wall with my eyes closed. Then I turned around and unlocked my phone and went to my texts. Allie wanted to know if I was in trouble or if my mom was mad. I didn't message her back because I didn't want to wake her up. And she didn't talk about her mom much so I don't know if she is the kind of mom that holds her kids phone at bedtime. A lot of moms do that. I feel like I have a stomach bug, and I am so thirsty. I know that I should not have drunk my mom's vodka. I am glad that you won't be reading this because I want my mom to like Allie. She is really fun.

I am going to go downstairs and get some water. I hope that OP doesn't bark and wake anyone up.

Deven

After Mom left my room, I text Zory. Then I delete it. Then I text her again. Then I delete it. Then I finally managed to send: *Hey Z. I had fun. Want to do homework together tomorrow?* Before I knew it, the *swuuup* sound of a sent text sounded. I could kick myself. Why did I ask her to hang out again so soon? I look like a loser.

hi! I had so much fun 😄
yes. I could always use homework inspiration 📖
what time should I come over?

> *how about 1:00? I have practice*
> *in the morning*

K. What's your address?

> *1030 N. Orianna*

see you tomorrow 🩶

The red heart emoji surprises me, like something just hit me in the head. I feel like I could run a marathon, but I really need to get to sleep. I have to be at the gym tomorrow at eight. I text Oliver.

hey Ol

hey

need a ride to practice?

yeah

I'll get you at 7:30 and we can hit Wawa for drinks and food

sounds good

see ya

I get under the covers and look at my phone one more time, hoping for another text from Zory, but that would be weird and random. So I turn my phone over and close my eyes.

***

"Bat Out of Hell" plays from my phone, and I roll over to shut the alarm off. It's seven o'clock. I just lie quietly and listen. I head out of my room and then press my ear to Mom's door. I gently open it and see Mom curled up on her bed asleep with the dog next to her.

OP knows the drill. He jumps down and comes to me, and I quietly shut the door behind him. I head downstairs and let him out back. Then I get something to drink, and I hear Julia in the den. I head to the kitchen, get a Gatorade from the fridge, and go and sit next to her on the couch. I hold out the bottle to her.

"Want a sip?" She barely shakes her head no, and I add, "You should drink some. You're probably dehydrated from throwing up so much."

She begrudgingly takes the Gatorade and gulps half of it, leaving a red ring around her mouth.

Anna Picari

"Is Mom awake?"

I shake my head and mentally thank God. I do a quick survey around the downstairs and also take a quick listen at the stairs. I then sit back down next to Jules. "I'm not going to say anything to Mom about your drinking her vodka. I hope you know that."

She looks at me like she's going to cry with relief.

"Oh my God, Deven. Thank you!"

"You can trust me. And if you ever want to talk about anything, I'll listen. Okay?" I say, and she throws both arms around my neck and hugs me hard. I don't know what the big deal is. Isn't that what a big brother is for?

Kim

I sleep in on Sunday. Usually, I get up around 6:00 on weekends, but when I roll over, my clock reads 7:28. What the heck? This is equivalent to getting up at noon for me. I roll onto my back, raise my hands over my head, and let out a big yawn. Where is OP? My eyes trail over my bed and then across my room. He's not here. One of the kids, most likely Deven, must have cracked my bedroom door to get him out. I'm so grateful for him. He's such a good kid. I find my fluffy white robe and UGG slippers and head downstairs.

Optimus Prime meets me at the foot of the stairs, wagging his fluffy tail but looking his age. Sometimes OP has the energy of a puppy, but mostly, he just lays around and wants to make us happy. I sit on the second to the bottom step and pull him into a hug. This dog likes hugs, which was therapeutic for me during my grief and is still helpful. There's nothing like the affection of a dog to lift your spirits. However, my "spirits" do not need lifting on this sunny winter day. Just as I notice a ray of sunlight coming in through the kitchen windows, I think I hear my children's voices. I hoist myself up with the railing and smile because they're just chatting—not fighting—and follow the melodious sound.

"Hello, beautiful children."

"Hi, Mom," Deven replies, and then Julia quickly echoes him. I ask them if they want pancakes, but Deven says that he has to get changed and head to practice as he gets up and gives me a side hug before hurrying upstairs. In record-breaking time, Deven is out the door, leaving me with Julia, who I notice doesn't look right. I ask her if she feels okay.

"Yeah. I'm fine, Mom, just not hungry," she replies. Then adds, "Maybe later, if that's okay."

"Of course it's okay. Just let me know when you're hungry. Did you have fun last night?"

Julia hesitates and then says, "Yesss! I'm glad that Allie and I are friends."

I smile in response and give her a hug and head to get dressed. She smells weird, but I quickly forget about that because I'm focused on wanting to get in a workout this morning.

The day flies by, and I'm thrilled that my hair still looks good from the blowout the day before, but I panic when I realize that my only set of sex-worthy underwear is dirty. I pull the bra and panties off the floor and smell the bra. It's good. The panties, not so much. I wash the crotch in the bathroom sink and use my hair dryer to dry it. I haven't performed a move like this since I was in college. I feel the muscles in my face forcing my mouth into a huge smile as I feel gratitude that Shawn did not see my bra or panties the night before.

Deven

I pick up Oliver, and we grab food and then head to the gym. I make the mistake of asking him if he would be able to play at Regionals. He replied with something that was a cross between a grunt and a sneer. Was it a yes or a no? I had no idea and was not in the mood to press him, but he did say that he's allowed to practice with us today, which I take as a good sign. I know that the team is all up in each other's business and I don't want Oliver to be embarrassed. They have classes with Oliver and know that he looks like he's basically in a coma most days.

Sometimes, I want to pull his iPad out of his backpack and physically make him do his work. I would be happy to help, but I know that he'd think that I was being douchey.

I pull into a faculty spot in front of the gym and grab my phone from the cupholder. I have a text from Z.

> *I made cookies for*
> *our study sesh* 🍪

🍪 ☺

🩶

What the fuck is up with that yellow heart emoji? I want to delete it from existence! I need to get a grip. It probably doesn't mean anything.

Oliver is walking slightly ahead of me because I was half walking and half texting. I see him look over his left shoulder and I say, "Sorry. Zory."

"Oh yeah. How did it go last night?'

I'm sure my face has a stupid grin across it as I answer. "Good. We're studying together today."

"Is that what you kids are calling it these days?" Oliver asks mockingly. And I just push him, and he laughs, and we head into the gym.

Kim

Zory O'Dell knocks on the door, and OP goes crazy. He barks like he's a guard dog, but I have no delusion that if someone were to break into the house, he would do nothing more than submissively urinate. OP is more of a couch potato these days, and while I appreciate his feeble efforts to protect us, I have realistic expectations of his abilities. I nudge him away and say hello as I open the door for Zory. I know that it's strange for the students to see me outside of school, so I try extra hard to be warm and welcoming when I encounter them out of what they believe is my natural habitat. She has a carryout container in her hands, and I ask if she made something delicious.

"I made cookies. Oatmeal raisin cookies. Everyone says they're delicious," Zory says enthusiastically. I don't know Zory well, but I really like her energy. She has an easy and warm way about her, which I admire especially because she comes from one of the wealthiest families at Freedom.

"May I try one?" I ask, knowing full well that Deven hates anything oatmeal and that he'd rather not have a cookie at all before eating an oatmeal raisin. Obviously, they have not had the "what's your favorite cookie?" conversation.

Zory pulls off the red top, and I select a cookie. I take a big bite.

"This is delicious, Zory! Wow!" I say honestly. It's a good cookie, but I think I may also just be hungry. I've been feeling nervous about my upcoming date and only had Greek yogurt with strawberries and three cups of coffee.

"Thanks, Ms. O," she says with a shy smile.

I yell for Deven, and he comes down the stairs as if the house were on fire. I guess that he doesn't want me to spend too much time with Zory in the inevitable event that I say something embarrassing.

"Hey Zory. Let's go upstairs," Deven says breathlessly, and he takes her hand and leads her and the cookies (much to my dismay) to his room.

I spend the afternoon doing some meal prep: baking chicken, chopping veggies, and creating hearty salads. This makes a few easy and nutritious dinners for the week. I then catch up on the wash. The washer is not empty when I open the lid, so I reach down and pull the wet garments out to toss into the dryer. But Julia's clothes from last night are in there with some bathroom towels. That's weird. I'll ask Jules about it later. I start my wash and go up to my office to answer my emails. Forty-five minutes later, I'm back in the basement folding the towels and Julia's clothes. And I remember that I forgot to ask her why they were in the wash while I put my wet clothes in the dryer.

Julia is in the living room, doing something on her iPad, wearing her AirPods. OP gets down from his spot on the couch and walks up to me. This brings Julia to attention.

"Hi, Mom."

"Hey, Jules. Why were the clothes you wore yesterday in the wash?" I ask, and I'm not sure if Julia's flinch was real or my imagination.

"Oh. I spilled something on myself and didn't want it to stain, so I threw the clothes in the wash. Deven must have started it when he washed his towels," Julia responded smoothly.

"I didn't see any stains, so you're good to go. I'm going out tonight so Deven can Uber Eats something for you guys."

Julia loves choosing food from an app. It's weird that she picks the same items from the grocery store or from our usual restaurants, but she selects her meals from the Uber Eats app slowly and meticulously and boldly.

Julia looks like she's thinking about the myriad restaurants that deliver to us but quickly snaps her head and looks at me. "Where are you going?"

Oh crap. The distraction didn't work.

Nonchalantly, I say, "I'm going to dinner with Shawn." But I am well aware that this is a big deal for me. This is a massive change in our family dynamic, and I feel guilty. My kids have never known a mom who was not home or who made plans on the fly.

But when I look at Jules, it doesn't seem like she's even listening to me, and she just tells me to have fun and goes upstairs, which I find suspicious.

Deven

Zory holds her backpack and then sits on the floor next to it. She pulls out her pre-calculus book first and asks, "If this is *pre*-calculus, what does *actual* calculus look like?"

I laugh because I feel the same way.

"I think my cousin took something like Calculus 3 at Ohio State. I asked her what *that* looked like, and she jokingly told me that she couldn't remember much of it due to the PTSD, but she did remember that it was the only C she received."

Zory just shakes her head and laughs. Then I laugh, too.

About two hours into our sesh, Zory stands up and asks if she can use the bathroom. I point to the door next to Julia's room. As she passes Julia's room, I hear her say, "Hey," and then Jules says something back as she enters the bathroom. *Shit*, I think. I hope I flushed the toilet the last time I was in there.

I take the opportunity to run downstairs and get two waters, two cans of Pepsi—one regular and one diet—and napkins. I intend to suggest we take a cookie break, but when I get back to my room, she's on the floor with the cookie container open and one in her mouth. It's the first time I've ever been jealous of a cookie.

But before I could lose control of my body and mind, Zory tells me that my phone was vibrating. I grab a cookie and take a bite. If I had to rank cookies, oatmeal raisin would be a smidge above a Fig Newton, but the cookie in my mouth is magic. Okay. Maybe not magic, but the fact that she made it propelled oatmeal to the top cookie spot.

I must be thinking too much about cookies because Zory asks me if I'm going to see who texted me. I pick up my phone from its spot on the bed and see that I have one text from my buddy Jackson and two from Oliver. Jack sent me a stupid meme, and Oliver wants to know how the hangout with Zory is going. I quickly like the meme from Jackson, and I tell Oliver that I will text him later. I roll back onto my butt on the floor and grab another cookie.

Zory snatches the cookie from my hand, and I immediately try to get it back. She falls back on the floor and shoves the entire cookie in her mouth while laughing hysterically. I grab a napkin, hold it under her mouth, and repeat "Spit it out" like Mom used to say to Julia when she shoved too much food in her mouth. Zory just laughs and keeps shaking her head no until her only two options are to spit it out or choke on it. She spits it into the napkin in my hand and continues laughing. I eventually hand her a water bottle, and she takes a big sip. She then uses the back of her hand to wipe her mouth. And it's suddenly quiet.

I don't know what prompts me, but I kiss her. She kisses me back, and I could not do basic addition if I were asked to right now because all my brain cells quickly move to my dick.

After a few minutes, hours, or days, I no longer have any sense of time. Zory breaks away and just looks at me. It's like she can see through me. Her lips are puffy, but her eyes look happy. I cannot control myself. I pull her onto my lap and start all over again. She's all in.

I move my hands up and down her back and then find them in the gray area under her arms but not yet on her boobs. Mom's voice is in my head, reminding me to always get consent, and I whisper, "Is this okay?" to her, and she says yes. I move my hand to the front of her shirt and gently touch her left boob. It's the first time I have ever felt one, and I think I may pass out, but her lips on my lips help that feeling pass.

She moves her lips to my ears and lets out a soft moan as she uses her tongue to circle the inside and outside of my ear. I begin to move my hand under her shirt when I hear Julia outside my room. I literally jump up and lift Zory up with me. It's like someone dumped a bucket of freezing cold water on us. We didn't close the door, which we seem to have remembered at the same time. And as I peek outside the door, I see Jules sneaking back into her room.

When I turn to Zory, she's sitting on the floor, leaning against my bed, smiling. I plop down next to her and grab her left hand. She squeezes my hand, and I squeeze back. Finally she says, "I think we really need to get some work done." I mumble some sort of agreement, and we go back to our math homework.

Julia

Entry 8

Mr. Jabs, I have been snapping and texting with Allie all day. We are talking about school and sending each other memes and she told me what Newark, New Jersey, is like. It sounds awesome because it's close to New York City. Have you ever been there? I haven't been anywhere except the shore, Disney World, and Italy. My Pops and Gram took us to Rome when I was 6, but I don't remember much about it. I think it was boring. The pictures we have all look the same. They have a lot of ugly paintings and a lot of churches. I would like to go to New York, I think. Maybe I will see if Mom will take me and Allie during spring break. Anyway, I have to finish my homework. I have to make a PowerPoint for the book <u>A Wrinkle in Time</u>. See????? I underlined the title of the book. Bye for now.

Kim

Shawn picks me up and we head to a local bar called Gingers. It's quiet because it is a Sunday evening, and I am relieved. Although I really love Freedom's parents, I always come off a little socially inept when I run into them "in real life," and I try not to talk about school things when I'm not there. Several of the teachers are neighborhood friends with some of the parents so the fraternization rules are laxed. I am grateful for this as I look at Shawn.

Gingers is the kind of bar that is . . . relaxed. A little grungy but has the best bar food within miles. The adorable server with blonde hair pulled back and very interesting tattoos displayed on both arms takes our drink order. Shawn and I maintain what I now believe are our usual drinks—Yuengling and vodka. We make idle chitchat as we open our menus. Our drinks arrive without fanfare, and we both order cheeseburgers and fries. Although I am considerably less nervous today, I never want to appear complicated or unnecessarily expensive.

Two finished drinks and two burgers later, we both order coffee. Time flies. Shawn is funny and interesting, a good storyteller. I admire that gift. When I'm relaying an amusing anecdote, I never tell it in order and have to stop and start again and I think people stop listening. Shawn, though, can make a tale vivid and touchable and, often, pee-your-pants funny.

After Gingers, Shawn opens the car door for me and suggests more "coffee" at his house. Aubrey and Oliver are at a primetime Eagles game. I hesitate for only a minute. I know what this means. Am I ready? I may need something stronger than coffee. "Sure," I reply. "Wine instead?" Shawn bends down and kisses me before I get into the Tesla.

Once there, we park in the hideaway driveway in the back of the house. I have only experienced his house from the vantage point of the front door when I would walk down to gather Deven from playdates with Oliver. I pause when I think that must have been close to ten years ago!

Following his lead, we both kick off our shoes in the laundry room, which is adjacent to the garage. As we walk into his home, I am struck by the emptiness of the house. It's beautiful but it looks as if it's staged for sale, with very few personal items around. It's a combination of contemporary and art deco. After we shed our coats, we head into his kitchen, which is surprisingly masculine. Dark wood and black stainless appliances highlight a huge concrete countertop. I take a seat at one of the barstools as he reaches into his wine rack for a bottle. He holds one up. "Red okay?" I nod, and he pours us each a glass.

He leads me to the den, which is just off the kitchen, and we sit on a cream-colored sectional. As I look around his home, sipping delicious wine, I decide that my New Year's resolution will be to redecorate my home. It just never seemed vital because we don't have a lot of visitors or entertain much. Shawn then asks me if I'm okay, and I quickly snap out of my HGTV trance.

"Honestly, I'm nervous." However, I am also slightly weirded out being in a home that contains an ex-wife, but I keep this to myself.

"Honestly, me too. I haven't been with anyone since well before the divorce," Shawn shares.

"I haven't been with anyone since Matthew died," I trump, and Shawn's eyes widen with questions that I don't feel like answering, so I simply take a graceful slug of my wine and then put the glass on the coffee table.

                                                    Anna Picari

I turn my body to face him and slowly kiss him. Shawn gracefully puts his glass on the end table, which I hadn't even noticed was there.

Within seconds, we're going at it like teenagers, and then Shawn takes my hand and leads me down to his bedroom. This move embarrassingly reminds me of a time that I hooked up with a guy from Theta Chi in his disgusting frat-house bedroom, but fortunately for me, Shawn's space is nicely decorated and smells faintly of his cologne.

Shawn pulls me down on the bed, and I hoist his sweater over his head to find that he's wearing a crisp, light blue T-shirt. He reaches under my shirt, then under my bra, and when his hand touches my nipple, I let out an involuntary moan. He removes his hand and leans back on his knees. "You okay with this?" he asks, and I reply that I am fine with all of it!

He presses me back onto the bed and then unbuttons my jeans, lowers the zipper, and pulls them off, taking my thong with them. I fumble with his belt and he assists me. I remove his jeans and can see the hardness struggling to get out of his boxers. I teasingly trace the length with my finger as I circle my tongue along his lips, neck, and ears. He moans appreciatively and reaches up to pull off my shirt. His mouth finds mine again, and he feels behind me for my bra hook. I move his hand to the clasp, located at the front of my bra, and he aptly unclasps it. He gathers both of my breasts in his soft and capable hands and uses his tongue.

Shawn bites and kisses until I feel like I will pass out if he doesn't touch between my legs. I am slightly cognizant of my hand on his boxers and reach inside to grab his dick. I start stroking, and he pauses only to pull them off and reposition himself between my legs. He uses what I am quickly learning must be a magical tongue to lick my clit into oblivion. I don't even know when I let go of him and grab the sheets with both hands. I raise myself to his tongue. Shawn puts his lips directly under my clit and sucks. I cry out "Fuck me now!" as I orgasm. He peeks out between my legs, and I smile at him. He climbs over me, grabs a condom from his nightstand, and kisses me. The taste of me on his lips is super sexy, and I don't even notice him placing the condom on his swollen shaft. He rolls over and pulls me on top of him. Shawn is looking directly at me, with his hands on my ass as I move up and down. Within minutes, he moans and shudders and pulls my upper body down to cover his.

We just lie there in a tender, postcoital hug. After a few minutes, I throw my shirt over my non-bra-ed breasts and headed to retrieve our wine glasses. I pad into the kitchen and grab the wine and pause for a second, relieved that my parts still work. Thoughts of Matthew flitter into my mind but I gently push them aside as I head back to Shawn. I refill both glasses, and we sit in mutual and comfortable silence for a while and then, without any words, we go at it again.

Kim

When I got home last night, the kids were in their rooms. Deven peeked out with a quick greeting when he heard me come up the stairs. I was happy to find Julia sound asleep when I looked in her room. It was barely nine o'clock, but I was still on a mild sex high, so I wanted a few minutes to gather myself and take a long shower.

As the warm water rained down, my brain replayed the events of the evening. Then came a feeling of indescribable shame, because I had cheated on Matt. Matt, the kind, handsome, funny, smart man whom I had vowed to be faithful to. I thought back to our first time. It was after our fourth date, and we'd gone to his place. I recall feeling nervous because I really liked Matt and anticipated having sex with him from the day we met. Needless to say, it was lovely because the lovemaking was gentle and loving. Tears started, and I slid to the shower floor, pulled my knees into my chest, and grieved the loss of that time and especially the loss of a good man, my lovely and loved husband.

This morning, I pull my hair into a low ponytail because I didn't blow it dry last night since I was emotionally wrecked. I wasn't going to wash it, but I feared that it may have smelled like sex. Both of the kids were quiet when I came downstairs, and OP was eating his breakfast. I admired his appetite for an old dog, his fur looking grayer than ever.

"Thanks for feeding the dog, whichever one of you did it," I say cheerfully.

"That was Jules, but I let him out," Deven replies.

"Then, thanks to both of you," I comment as I suggest that Deven drive to school so he can drive himself home from practice afterward. I tell him to park in my spot, and I'll park in another spot.

Julia pipes up. "Can I go with him? Please!!"

I look at Deven, and he gives a shoulder shrug that indicates he doesn't mind. I say that I don't mind, but I do—a little. Or maybe a lot.

Memories that I keep at a distance quickly resurface and wash over me like a tsunami.

"There's been an accident."

"We're very sorry to have to tell you that your husband has passed."

"Somebody take the baby."

I was vaguely aware that I was holding a baby and was being told that my husband was dead.

I'd had a relatively peaceful labor and delivery, and Matt was on his way to my parents' house to retrieve Deven. We were so excited for Deven to meet his new sister. But Matt never made it. A tractor trailer carrying baby furniture blew a red light, and Matthew was unable to stop before the truck T-boned the side of his car. The gruesome irony of it being a baby furniture delivery truck was not lost on me and, weirdly, I think about that scene in the PBS series *Downton Abbey*. It was art imitating *my* life.

My ability to get in a vehicle, turn it on, and go somewhere is the result of several years of intense therapy. However, my therapy never covered future driving episodes involving throwing my children to the vehicular wolves.

"Sure, Jules," I say in an unconvincing voice, but she doesn't notice. Since all of Julia's transportation needs are met via Muber (Mom Uber) or GUber (grandparent Uber), my fear of motor vehicle accident moves back into my brain. Two years after Matt's accident, I was heading to the grocery store and a car stopped without warning in front of us. I had to slam on my brakes, stopping within centimeters of the car. I drove home immediately and called my therapist the next day.

Anna Picari

With a thumping heart, I gently remind Deven that he is now responsible for transporting not just one but both of my most valued things in the world. I give them both kisses and tell them that I will see them later.

On my solo drive to work, I choose to think about the hickey currently staining my left breast and how much I look forward to seeing Shawn again.

Deven

Julia and I finished breakfast and put our dishes in the sink before heading out twenty minutes after Mom. Once we're on the road, Jules asks me if I like Zory. I tell her to mind her own business, but she doesn't stop. I finally answer that I do, in fact, like her. She is cool, smart, and funny. Julia adds that she is also hot, and I cannot argue there. My mind takes me back to Saturday night, and I quickly redirect my thoughts so that I calm the beginning of an erection.

Zory and I have been texting nonstop and have plans to go out next weekend. We decided to keep it on the down-low at school. I don't want anyone to ask me any questions, and neither does she. Since I don't usually see her often in the halls, I can't wait for Spanish.

Julia

Entry 9

Hey, Mr. J. Silent homeroom today so I thought that I'd write. I know we have to have at least 10 entries. I got in later today because I rode with Deven. He is a cool brother, and I feel much cooler walking into school with him than with my mom. Everyone seems to know Deven. I think that he is popular. I wish I was popular. Maybe people will notice me because I am now friends with Allie. I know that we are new friends, but I can tell she is cool. Her hair is shiny and blonde. My hair is plain brown. But everyone says that I have pretty eyes. That's just because they are light green, and no one has that color. Mom says that I have my dad's eyes. There are only 3 pictures of me with my dad and I am a new baby in all of them. Sometimes I miss him. Is it weird to miss someone that you never really met? There's the bell. TTYL

Deven

It's the middle of APUSH, and a girl named Vanessa sends me a message on my iPad.

what's up with you and Z?

> *what do you mean?*

you know what I mean

> *do not know. We went out and
> then did homework*

do you like her?

> *why r u asking?*

she's my friend!!
I don't want her to get hurt

> *why would I hurt her?*

Idk

I sort of like that Zory is talking about me to her friends. I hope that it means that she likes me. I try to put this out of my mind. I really want an A in this class. I think about college more than my friends do, but I'm hoping to go somewhere really good, like MIT or Princeton. Rumor has it that someone is more likely to get into Princeton if they live in the Midwest or on the West Coast, but I don't care. My GPA is golden, and I am taking the SAT and ACT soon and need to try to find time to study for them. I just have so much work and extracurricular responsibilities. I tell myself it'll all work out.

Kim

The first half of this March day flew by with the normal amount of drama with only one exception: I was called to the first grade classroom because a student had put his tongue in the opening of his water bottle, and it wasn't coming out. The school nurse and Mandy tried for several minutes and then decided to call the EMT and his parents. The poor child was hysterical. I squatted down next to him and told him that he would be okay. I asked him to squeeze my hand as much as it hurt. He squeezed tightly. I put my arm around him and then opened the Disney+ app on my phone. I let him choose a movie. That was the distraction he needed. A few minutes later, his mom arrived at the same time as the paramedics. The student was whisked off to Temple University Children's Medical Center in an ambulance with a paramedic holding the suctioned water bottle.

And now the second half of today begins with my scheduled check-in with Oliver McDaniel, which I have a feeling will turn into a full session complete with a PowerBar and bag of Fritos from my snack stash. When I checked his student portal, I found that he had several incomplete assignments. When he arrives at my office, he sits on my couch without me asking him. I think he senses that I am very concerned, but he also looks like he doesn't want to talk. He has dark circles under his eyes and he's weighing something out in his mind.

I open the conversation. "Oliver, I think there's more than you're letting on."

"I know that you're, like, dating my dad or whatever. I don't want you telling him anything."

I point to the sign on my coffee table:

What you say in here, stays in here unless:
Someone is hurting you
You want to hurt someone
You want to hurt yourself
You give me permission to share what we
talk about with another trusted adult

Oliver reads it and appears to be deliberating. He says okay and that he needs a minute. He opens his mouth to say something and then closes it. Finally, he says that he's worried about his mom.

"What are you worried about specifically?" I pry gently.

"I know that she drinks too much, but I don't know if it's that or if she's doing something else or if she's sick."

I ask him what makes him think she's using, and Oliver tells me that at the Eagles games the night before, Aubrey left him for over an hour. And then she texted Oliver and asked what section they were in. Oliver told her and kept his eyes on the stairs and finally spotted her. "Ms. O, she looked like a zombie. I went down and got her. And we were sitting in the middle of the row, and she could not get to her seat without falling over every person we had to get past."

I take a deep breath to center myself. He may be right. "Did she get to enjoy the rest of the game at least?" I already know the answer.

"She went missing for a long time. I mean, almost a whole quarter. Then she fell asleep. Who does that at an Eagles game? It's so fucking loud. Uh, sorry about the f-word."

I tell him that it's fine. Then I ask him if he told his dad. Oliver says that he was thinking about it because he's really worried about her. He adds, "She only has us. Me and Dad."

I support his plan to talk to his dad, and he seems a little lighter as he gets ready to leave my office. I tell him that we'll talk tomorrow and that he can come and see me whenever he needs.

After Oliver leaves, I have a sinking feeling. This is a sad and complicated situation for that poor boy.

Part II

April–June

Julia

Entry 10

So, Mr. J., I have been thinking about the thing that Allie does. You know what I'm talking about. She cuts. With a razor. I try to think about how she does it and how it feels and what happens. Part of me wants to try it, but I'm afraid. It hurts when I get needles at the doctor, and I hate it when I have a cavity. One time, Mom, Deven, and I were riding our bikes in Fairmount Park. I was around 7 years old and really slow at bike riding. But I wanted to be as fast as Deven, so I made up my mind to catch up.

I used all my power to pedal as fast as possible and was almost near Deven and my bike went flying and I landed on the hard bike path. I remember a lot of blood and crying a lot. I still have a scar on my knee. Mom told me that I was riding on some wet leaves that were on the path and my wheels spun out. That makes sense. But it really hurt, and I didn't like that, and I don't like bleeding. Allie says that she does not feel anything, but I think she is lying. But I hope not because I trust Allie, and I can't trust someone who lies. But now I think that I am a liar too. Remember that time I got drunk and Mom didn't find out? That's kind of a lie, right? I feel bad about that. I feel wrong about a lot of things.

Oliver

I wonder if people ever feel like they're alone. I mean completely alone, inside and out. Like there are all these people around them and they can't connect with any of them. Sometimes I feel like a ghost, just swaying in between humans while they look right through me.

I have been seeing Ms. Orsetti a lot. I even let her tell my dad that she thinks that I need to see a therapist outside of school. My dad tried three therapists, and none of them were taking new clients. He told me that he would ask "Kim" if she had any references. My dad and "Kim" have been together since January. She's really nice, but it's still weird when I come home and they're watching something on Netflix with a bowl of popcorn between them. I didn't know my dad even knew how to make popcorn. Before Ms. O came around, we microwaved Pop Secret. Now, my dad has a special pot, organic peanut oil, and popcorn kernels. It tastes better, but it's weird. They always invite me to watch whatever they're watching with them. How awkward would that be? Just once, I want to move the popcorn bowl that's between them and plant my ass in its spot. But I would never do that.

My dad seems happy. Him and Mom were always fighting. I think it started before I was born when things were hard because dad had to be at the hospital all the time. Or maybe my mom was the problem like she is now. I try to help her as much as I can. I bring her food and make sure she has enough water. Don't get me wrong, she has good days. She takes a shower, gets dressed, and takes walks. She attempts to cook a meal, and I eat it and pretend that it's delicious. This seems to make her happy.

I sometimes think that if I am just *better*, she will be better, too. I managed to get my grades up enough to play in the final basketball game. I made 18 points, but we still lost. My mom came to that game, and I wanted her to be proud of me, to sort of know that I was dedicating the game to her. Ms. O says it doesn't work that way and that I am already good enough. But I want her to get better for me because I exist on the face of the Earth. I am here—her own flesh and blood. I am almost afraid to go away to college because who will take care of her? I think my dad is at the end of his rope with her. If he gives up on her, where would she go? She'll be all alone except for me. And I am barely surviving, barely alive.

I get wanting to stay lost because now I can't feel anything else, but I agree to go to the park with some of the guys. Someone's older brother got us two cases of beer, and I am happy to partake. I chug three beers in a row, finally getting that dizzy, sleepy buzzed feeling. I am talking to my bro, Jayson, when suddenly, another guy I don't know makes some comment about us being fags. I'm not sure what happens to me, but I feel anger. Not just normal anger. Anger that comes from my feet and shoots straight to my fists. You know how old people use the expression "I saw red" when they describe getting pissed? I'm not seeing red; I'm seeing white. Bright white. White that can blind a guy. And before I know it, I break my beer bottle and am trying to slash the guy. It takes four guys to hold me back as the beer guy says, "Yo. It was just a joke, bro."

This makes me want to charge him again. "Fuck you!" I shout. "Fuck you. Don't ever use that fucking word near me again, asshat."

I hate that word because it's offensive to people who are gay. It's just offensive. And that guy is a complete, ignorant dick.

Deven

Zory and I are official. And I feel how a celebrity must feel. People look at us when we walk to lunch together. If I'm alone, I notice people whispering. People with cameras are everywhere hoping to get a picture of us together.

Nah, just kidding. But that would be awesome though. Zory looks amazing in pictures.

And in person.

And naked.

Yes to that. I have seen her naked. A lot.

We haven't gone all the way yet, but we're pretty close. I don't know how much longer I can get by with just a hand job. Z is worth waiting for.

I'm having a great year. With the exception of how the basketball season ended (we lost at Regionals), things are going my way. My GPA was 4.4 at the end of last semester, and I smoked the February ACT *and* the March SAT. Thank you very much. My school counselor thinks that I have a good shot at getting into my top choices if I keep my grades up.

The only thing bringing me down a little is Oliver. He could be on a poster for depression or teen suicide. I try to talk to him, and we still hang out. Last weekend we went to Rittenhouse Square and got food at Pizzeria Vetri. He seemed better, and we talked a little as we went in and out of random stores. Oliver told me that he's happy I'm with

Zory. He's had a few classes with her and thinks that she's the real deal. But I can tell that he's jealous. I guess I understand that. It used to be the two of us all the time and now it's not. Zory has a friend named Sophia, and I've talked to him about hanging out together. I think he's going to go for it.

Zory and I meet at her locker at the end of the day. It takes every bit of self-control not to start kissing her neck. God, she has the perfect neck. It's long and smooth.

"Hey there, Demonio!" Z says as she pulls me in for a tight hug.

"Hey there, Bronceada," I reply as I mentally try to control my hardening dick. *Stop thinking about her neck. Stop thinking about her neck.* It's not working fast enough, and I have to keep the hug going a little longer until it finally relaxes.

We talk about our homework a bit, and then Zory leaves because she has work. She has a seasonal job at Rita's Water Ice. She likes it a lot because her coworkers are cool but doesn't like when the bees come out and circle the window. Most people don't realize that Rita's started in Philly. Some guy started selling it on his front porch or some shit like that.

I text Oliver to see if he wants to get food or something.

want to go to Wawa or something?

I start walking to my locker as I wait for a response. I check my phone after I grab my jacket. A lot of high schools don't give kids lockers but Freedom does. And they make it stupidly clear that they can open our lockers at any time, for any reason.

Nothing from Oliver. I text again.

Yo Man

sorry yeah, let's get food.

meet me at my car.

Oliver is leaning against the car when I get to Mom's parking space. It's a prime spot because it's close to the main entrance. Mom has been parking in Mr. Hudson's spot since he is on paternity leave for a few months. I don't like people seeing me pull in or out but it's okay. At least I don't have to drive home with Ms. Orsetti.

"My man," I say as I give Oliver a side hug.

"Where do you want to go?" he asks.

"I don't care. I'm just hungry."

"Mickey D's?" he suggests.

I head to McDonald's drive-thru. I order two Quarter Pounders with Cheese and a coke. Oliver orders a Big Mac Meal with a Sprite.

"What are you, a toddler? Who the fuck drinks Sprite?" I ask accusingly.

"A real man," Oliver answers.

"It tastes like ass."

"You would probably know."

And I punch his arm and call him a dick as I pull to the second window. Why does every McDonald's have two windows? You always have to wait at the second window anyway. It seems like a play on self-importance. Chick-fil-A only has one window, and the drive-thru line wraps around the building fourteen times.

I turn on Spotify as we head to our neighborhood. I pull in front of his house and ask him if he wants to hang. Oliver looks nervously at his house and says, "Nah. I got shit to do."

Shit is code for "I don't know what my mom is up to." Oliver tries to cover for his mom, but I know things are bad. I hardly ever see her, and she seems to take a lot of naps. Although Oliver never said anything to me, I think she's gone missing before.

Oliver has changed so much this year. He used to be a smartass goof, but now he's so serious all the time. I try to distract him as much as I can, but I have a life, too. As I pull in front of my house, a feeling of worry comes over me. Oliver is like my brother, and sometimes I feel like he's slipping away from me.

Anna Picari

Kim

Julia waits on the couch in my office, playing with one of the Easter Bunny plush pillows that adorn my couch as I finish sending emails. I look up from my laptop and see her texting away. She is beautiful. I imagine she'll be one of the lucky middle schoolers who will bypass the awkward stage. I'm continuously struck by her resemblance to her dad. Her dark hair and green eyes, surrounded by thick dark lashes, placed perfectly on her genetically dominated Sicilian skin. All of Matthew's grandparents came from Sicily, and his parents met at a parish mixer. His grandparents called him Matteo. I had the privilege of knowing all four of his grandparents because they lived until their late eighties, early nineties. This always gave me comfort because I believed that it was some kind of cosmic insurance that Matthew would live to a ripe old age. Boy, was I naive.

I close my laptop, and this gets Julia's attention. "Can we go now?" she asks expectantly.

"Yep."

"Oh, good. I have to finish my World History."

I tell her that I don't feel like cooking and ask if she wants to go out for an early dinner.

"Can we just get takeout?"

I am disappointed. I was hoping for some quality alone time with my daughter. But I say sure, tell her to pick a place, and ask her to text Deven to get his order.

Twenty-five minutes later, we arrive home carrying a pepperoni pizza from Mario's and an order of their famous truffle fries. I pour myself a glass of red and pull out paper plates. I hear Deven's door open and then his feet heading downstairs. *Thump, THUMP. Thump, THUMP.* Deven has always come down the stairs in the same descending rhythm. Light foot, hard foot. And I smile with love for him as he grabs a slice, folds it, and takes a big bite.

"This is it for me. Oliver and I got food after school, and I'm still full," Deven says with a mouth full of pizza.

A feeling of unrecognized relief comes over me. Something about Oliver's mood is not sitting right with me. I mentioned therapy to Shawn several times, both professionally and personally. I have also given him names of therapists I trust. He continually says that he's looking into it, and I have to bite my tongue from saying something snarky. This is one of those times where my being the school social worker and my being Oliver's dad's girlfriend collide. I am leery about offering Shawn parenting advice, but as a social worker, I'm frustrated by his lack of concern.

Deven sits next to Jules at the counter, where she's covering her slice with truffle fries. I grab my wine and a slice and sit next to her, taking a fry off Julia's pizza and popping it into my mouth. She understands that I want her to save some fries for me, and she slides the aluminum takeout dish my way.

I take a long sip of wine as the kids talk about a Netflix show that they watch together. Honestly, I think Deven pretends to like the show just to spend time with his sister. I don't think Deven is very interested in the social lives of an Indian American girl and her friends. But regardless, it's sweet. They clean up their messes, and both head up to their rooms as I glance at my phone and discover three unread texts. The first one is from Mom asking me to call her. The second one is from Kana, and the last one is from Shawn. I call Mom because I know

                                                        Anna Picari

it will be a quick call. *Jeopardy* will be on any minute, and she and my dad never miss that. It's comical to watch them bellow out answers at the television.

"Kim, dear. Thanks for calling."

"Of course, Mom. What's up?"

Mom goes on to quickly tell me that she and Dad are heading to Atlantic City tomorrow for a few days at the Borgata Hotel Casino this weekend. I laugh because Mom always has to let me know where they go, when, and for how long. I'm not exaggerating. I can recall a text that said, "Dad and I are going to Jersey to get tomatoes. Talk to you when we get back." You can walk to Jersey from where we live. For real. I wouldn't, but I could. However, I believe my parents are just protecting my heart and assuaging the anxiety lurking just below the surface. They know I would be completely lost without them.

"Oh fun," I replied. "Good luck, and stay away from the weed dispensaries."

"Oh, you! Very funny, Kimmie."

We end the call with "I love you"s and hang up. I then call Kana. She tells me that she has to vent about her new coworker. I tell her to go for it and listen as she shares that said coworker was flirting shamelessly with her boss. I respond with appropriate bestie responses ("Ugh," "Are you freaking kidding," "What an A-hole") as she continues the rant with a diatribe about women who are taking all women down. I put in my AirPods as I walk upstairs to put on sweats, still listening to my friend Gloria Steinem. After about ten minutes, Kana is calmer, and we say goodnight. I then settle into bed to chat with Shawn.

I text:

Hey there 🩶

Hey babe. Free to talk?

Yep

My phone came to life with the "Old Phone" ring, and I answer on one and a half rings. "Hello?"

Shawn says, "Kimberly," with a smile in his voice, and I can't help but feel a stupid grin pass across my face. No one calls me Kimberly. It's only Kim and Kimmie.

"Are you home or at the office?"

"Office. Just finished my last appointment," Shawn replies as I look at the clock on my nightstand. 6:50 p.m. "It was crazy today. I didn't have time to eat lunch, so I hope that you don't mind if I munch on a PowerBar while we talk."

I laugh and tell him to "munch away" and share with him some of the nonconfidential minutiae of my day. He tells me about a four-year-old who came in with an orange Skittle up his nose. The conversation is easy. We make plans for the upcoming weekend, and just as I am ready to say goodnight, he says, "I have to tell you something." My heart goes into my stomach.

I give a nervous laugh and say, "In my experience, the words 'I have to tell you something' are rarely followed with 'you just won the lottery.'"

"No, no. It's nothing too nefarious. It's just that I'm going to be putting our divorce agreement into effect, and I'm worried about how Oliver is going to take it." I know what Shawn means. His divorce decree states that the house must be bought out by the other spouse, or else it must be sold outright.

"Are you buying Aubrey out?" I ask.

"No. This is too much house for just me and Oliver. I'm going to look for something smaller. By the time everything goes through, Oliver will be done with high school."

I don't say anything because I'm worried about Oliver. They have fifty-fifty custody now, but that won't matter in about a year when he turns eighteen. Oliver sees himself as Aubrey's caretaker and will most likely want to make her home his primary residence. If that happens, I fear his college dreams will change drastically.

Anna Picari

"Are you there?"

I snap out of it. "Yeah. I'm here. I'm just thinking about what will become of Oliver."

"He'll be fine. He will be on his way to Penn State and be free of the likes of us," Shawn says.

I think about what to say next. I have to be careful because I don't want to cross lines. "Umm, Shawn. Have you spoken to Oliver about all this?"

Shawn tells me that he's waiting to tell his son, but Aubrey likes the idea. Of course Aubrey likes the idea. Some of the houses in this neighborhood go for three-quarters of a million dollars. She'll have quite a bit of money in her hands to do God knows what. I decide to put it off for now and change the subject.

"I know you're ready to head home and have a more substantial meal, so I will let you go."

Shawn says goodnight and that he likes me very much. This is what he says to me because I'm not ready for the "I love you" part.

I'm not sure if I do love Shawn. Like Shawn? Sure. Attracted to Shawn? Absolutely! But I find myself comparing him to Matthew, and I know that's not fair. I don't know what Matthew would be like now, thirteen years older. But Matthew was my other half, the calm to my anxiety, the impulsiveness to my practicality. I don't believe in soul mates, but he was the perfect fit for me.

And now I'm crying. Damn. It still creeps up on me. Fucking grief.

When I was doing my MSW internship, I had a client who lost her six-year-old son to cancer. I found myself sitting silently during our sessions because I wasn't sure what to say to her while she wept. I brought this up with my supervisor, and she gave me several ways to move forward with this client. Additionally, we had a long discussion about losing someone you love. She told me that grief is the price you pay for loving someone completely. And until I lost Matt, I never understood how painfully true that is.

Kim

The weeks go by faster toward the end of the school year, and I shake my head in incredulity when I flip my day planner to May. I have a notation to plan a summer college tour for Deven. I was going to see if Oliver wanted to come, with or without a parent. Deven has a rock-solid list of colleges: Princeton, Penn State, Pitt, Temple, St. Joe's, and Villanova. I know that Princeton is his top choice, but any Ivy League school is a reach for 99.9 percent of students. Shawn told me Oliver wants to go to Penn State. Kana went to Penn State and still drags her children there for football games. She was furious at the university during the Paterno shit but found it in her heart to forgive and, again, proudly displays a We Are . . . Penn State magnet on her car. There's something both endearing and annoying about Penn State alum.

Things are going well with Shawn. We have compatible personalities and are in sync in the bedroom. Last weekend, I made dinner at my house because Deven was out with Zory and Jules was at Allie's. In the middle of dinner, Shawn reached across the table and lightly ran a finger down my arm, and next thing I knew, I was sitting at my kitchen table without a shirt on. Shawn managed to crawl under the table and reached up and unbuttoned my blouse and unhooked my bra. His mouth followed his fingers up my body and tasted as he went. He bit my shoulder, then my collarbone. He gently touched my right nipple, and not long after, his mouth followed. His tongue circled my right nipple while he pinched my left nipple. I arched my back and let out a sigh of ecstasy. Backing away for a second, he unbuttoned my pants and slid them down to the floor, taking my panties with them. He roughly opened my legs and started to taste. I muttered something about having to cum, and he said no while he continued to kiss between my legs. I kicked off my pants and panties and tried to stand. He grabbed my wrist and pulled me back onto the chair. I was writhing and moaning until he finally stood and led me to the couch and used his hand while he whispered in my ear, "Are you ready to cum?"

Breathlessly, I managed to say yes, and he brought me to the point of no return while deftly pulling off his pants and putting on a condom. After I climaxed, he laid down and pulled me on top of him. Honestly, I'm not sure how I was able to use my legs after that mind-blowing orgasm. I straddled him and rode for less than two minutes. He came quickly, and afterward, I remained on top of him for a few extra seconds, trying to enjoy the warmth of his body. Besides, I didn't want to be rude. *Thanks for the big O, but I don't really want to stay connected that long.*

The odd thing about us is that we usually get up and go about life like we didn't just do unspeakable things to one another. This night was not that different. We got dressed and sat back down at the kitchen table and finished the eggplant parm that I'd made.

Matt and I would lay together and most likely take a short nap after sex. I felt so much love and safety. I understood why the term *spooning* is used. We fit together, the front of his knees pressed into the backs of mine, my ass tucked into his groin, just like we were two spoons, perfectly contoured to fit neatly together.

I wonder . . . is this how I know I don't love Shawn? I don't care enough to lie there.

Deven

I can see the junior year finish line. I have four Advanced Placement tests coming up: Chem, English Comp, APUSH, and Statistics. I think that I will do okay, but I need to get a score of 5 on as many as I can. Princeton includes AP scores as part of the admission process. I applied for a job at Mario's as a busser. I like the vibe in there, and the people seem cool. Zory and I talk about senior year a lot. She talks like we'll still be together, and I'm happy about that. We see each other all the time now, but summer is coming. Her family goes to Nigeria for two weeks as soon as school ends.

Zory tells me about the beaches in Lagos. Her family meets there every June. Most of her mother's family is still there. Her grandparents come for a month in the spring, and other family members visit at random times. I have met her aunt and some cousins. They are really nice.

My whole family consists of like five people. That's not really true, but we don't really see anyone from my dad's side of the family. It would be weird to see them now anyway. They're complete strangers. My dad's parents send me birthday and Christmas gifts, but they only send Julia Christmas gifts. Mom told me about this when I was around ten. She throws my birthday cards in the trash because she thinks it's disrespectful to Jules. They've never visited. I think that's why I want to always be close to Julia. She may be all I have in the world as far as relatives go.

Mom is planning a college tour. Julia will stay with Pops and Gram. I think Oliver and Shawn may come with us. It will be so much fun.

Speaking of fun, Zory and I are finally setting up Oliver and Sophia this weekend. I think this may be the perfect distraction for Oliver. He's stressed out because his parents told him that they may be putting the house up for sale at the end of the summer. I think he's worried about where he'll live or where his mom will end up. He doesn't go into detail about the situation with his mom, but I can tell that it's not good. Oliver says things like, "My mom passed out on the El, and someone called 911. My dad and I had to go get her from Jefferson-Einstein Hospital. Good thing my dad knew some people there because they let us see her without a psych eval, whatever that means."

I know what that means. It means that someone thinks that she is a danger to herself and others. I know about this kind of stuff from Mom. She's the biggest advocate for mental health and does presentations at other schools and to parents. I think Mom is worried about Oliver's mental health. She always looks at him like she's trying to read his mind when he's around. I'm sure she'll be shrinking him the whole time we're on the college tour. But I like that she worries about Oliver. I do, too, and having her worry takes some of the pressure off me.

Oliver

I cannot fucking believe what I just heard. My parents are going to sell our house. I guess I knew that it was inevitable, but what the actual fuck? And I know it was my dad's idea. He probably wants a bachelor pad that he can use to screw Ms. O without mom being around and me being away at college. Doesn't my dad see that Mom needs us? She has fewer normal days and seems stoned most of the time. That is, if she's actually awake and able to have a conversation with us. I make sure she eats. Last week, she vomited all over herself, and when I helped her get changed, I saw weird marks on her arms. And there were bruises. I googled this, and it said that it was either leukemia or needle marks. It's fucked up that I hope she has leukemia, but I'm going to find a way to talk to my dad about it. All of his friends are doctors. What if that's her problem, and we're just being really judgy? I mean, sick people sleep a lot, too. And I read that certain types of leukemia are curable.

At times, I feel like I'm losing my shit. I feel like the world is crashing down on most days. I know my dad and Deven try to get me to lighten up, but it's hard. It's not like someone can tell me to look on the bright side and I'll have an epiphany and be like, "Oh my fucking god. That's all I have to do. I wish I knew this sooner. The bright side. Yeah. I'll look that way."

I bring up a therapist a lot to my dad, and he always says that he's working on it. It doesn't seem like he is. Whatever.

I'm trying to get in a good head space to go out with Deven, Z, and Sophia again. Sophia is really cool, and we had a good time hanging out. Ain't ready to hang with her alone, though. There are random times that I feel like I'm going to cry. I can't explain why. One time in English, I had to rush out of the room like I was going to shit myself if I didn't get to a bathroom asap. I got into the bathroom stall just as bullshit tears started. Like I said. I am falling the fuck apart. Plus, I'm nervous.

The only experience I have with a girl is when Livie Bates kissed me at a lame beer party in the woods in eighth grade. I just stood there like a statue or some shit like that. Livie walked away, and I just stood there. Fucking embarrassing. Like, everyone knows that I am a stone-cold introvert. My whole life, my dad, Mom, even Deven have tried to help me. Deven pulls me into conversations and includes me in social events. He tried to get me to go to prom last month, but there was no fucking way that was going to happen. What? I was just going to go with a rando or one of Zory's friends who didn't have a date. I imagined just sitting there stiffly, hoping she didn't want to dance with me. Deven got the message after several efforts to entice me to attend.

Sophia has been hanging in my mind rent-free, though, so I don't want to fuck this up.

Kim

The end of the year is my favorite time at work, but I don't say that aloud. My coworkers would not appreciate it. They have all kinds of mandatory but somewhat superfluous paperwork to complete while having to continue teaching lessons. Teaching is demanding! All Hail All Teachers. Forever! Amen.

However, as the school social worker, I close out files and feel successes in my heart when I know that a student has overcome an obstacle or worked hard and really learned to care about school and *graduates*! I cry every year at graduation because I am so proud of the kids. Knowing what I know about family situations, health issues, learning disabilities, neurodivergences, and other shit makes me want to cheer for those students. They never cease to impress and inspire me.

At home, it's a different story. I intentionally do my spring cleaning in May, and I busy myself wiping the ceiling fans and upper crown molding. I move and clean under furniture, shampoo carpets, and rearrange shelves. I go through closets and donate an excessive amount of outgrown clothing to St. Vincent de Paul.

All my cleaning is done while listening to an audiobook. I carefully choose my audiobooks to ensure there won't be any triggers in the story. I usually settle on hokey love stories where I know that the lonely baker will eventually get with the new, handsome architect who just arrived in town from the big city. It always fascinates me that when these types finally fall in love, they always have porno sex. It's never vanilla sex. It's as if they believe that the best sex must be reserved for "the one." I never believed that. I started to have sex when I was seventeen with my high school boyfriend. We were both virgins and floundered our way through. We did it every which way and everywhere. When I think about some of the things that we did—in the car while driving, mind you—I shudder. And I formally apologize to any commuters we may have inadvertently endangered.

I guess because my first experiences were so free and fun, I set the bar high. That's not to say that I didn't have sloppy, frat party sex in college just to get off, but I had several go-to guys who were down for anything. By the time I met Matthew, I knew how to get what I wanted from a man and how to give a man what he didn't even know he wanted. Matthew was a quick learner and then became a teacher. The best of both worlds. Plus, I loved him, body and soul.

Matthew's sense of spirit would have been all about our upcoming college visits because he was dedicated to his Villanova Wildcats. Oliver is coming with us without a parent, and I'm so happy. No pressure to occupy Shawn or Aubrey, and I can have clear eyes on Oliver. We're heading out in early June to visit Penn State and Pitt, staying overnight in Pittsburgh, and then heading to Happy Valley (eyeroll) in the morning. We'll visit Temple and St. Joe's the following week. Deven and I will visit Princeton and Villanova without Oliver. He's not planning on applying to either of those schools. But I'm pleased that we will be sharing a lot of car time together.

Shawn will be a distraction this summer, as well. I have shared my midsummer malady (as I call it), and he says that he understands. I think very few people can understand the feelings that accompany having a birth and a significant death on the same day, but I appreciate his effort. Just like I appreciate all of his efforts. On paper, Shawn is a great guy. He is romantic and generous, funny and smart. (Here's the *but* . . .) But lately, I feel bored with him. I know that sounds like a bitch-thing to say, but it's true. And I feel unappreciative of having someone who is committed to having a relationship with me.

The spark in the beginning may have just been my sexual cobwebs being swept away. Don't get me wrong, the sex is very fine, but we are not in our twenties, and I don't want to be the one to teach sexual connectedness or adventurousness anymore. I'm not going to make any decisions this month, though, that's for sure.

Deven

Three out of the four AP tests that I took were doable, but the APUSH test was an absolute mindfuck. There was simply not enough time to answer the questions. I can read and comprehend like a pro, but the test asked for too much. I hope I squeaked by with a 3. I feel so much relief that those tests are O-V-E-R! Huzzah! I shouldn't have to take any finals because I have A's in all my classes. That's a benefit for juniors and seniors. If you have an A average going into the final, you don't have to take the test. I plan on cruising until the end of the year. I'm still training with some teammates and helping with the final edition of the school newspaper. Oliver goes home right after school these days. I think he does that to check on his mom. I haven't been to his house recently, so I have no clue what her status is, and Oliver doesn't want to talk about it when I ask. So I've stopped asking.

Deven

Finally, Oliver agreed to go out with us and Sophia again. I like them together. Zory says they're a good fit.

I pick up Oliver and we drive to Zory's house to get her and Sophia. Oliver texts Z when we're almost there, and they meet us on the front stairs. Sophia looks like she put in extra work to look nice. I mean, she's always cute, but she looks borderline hot tonight. Zory looks like she always does—perfect. I think about her hand on me the minute I see her. We haven't gotten further than touching yet. I am dying to taste every part of her. I think I can do it right because I study the dudes in the videos that I watch.

The sound of a closing car door snaps me out of a sexual daydream. I unbuckle and turn around and give Z a kiss as she slides in the backseat behind me. Sophia gets in next to her and shuts the door. Oliver looks over his left shoulder and says hey to both girls. Zory's vanilla scent fills the car, and I inhale deeply.

Z asks where we're going, and I tell her we're heading to Rittenhouse Square. But then I back pedal and ask if everyone is okay with this plan. Sophia and Zory think it's a perfect idea. I'm happy the weather was a delightful 68 degrees, but I know it will get colder when the sun goes down. Both girls are fully Philly, so they have sweaters. I don't even bother looking for street parking and find a spot in the corner parking garage. It's Saturday night, and it's flocked.

We walk to Gran Caffe L'Aquila. This place reminds me of the cafés in Italy. It is that legit. The smell of fresh espresso and sweet gelato hits you as soon as you enter the store. We head to the middle of the café. Zory and Sophia order a cappuccino, I order a double espresso, and Oliver gets a bottle of San Pellegrino. I pay for Zory and pray that Oliver is paying attention. Thankfully, he is, and he covers Sophia's coffee. We get a small table outside the café and sit with our beverages, talking about the flavors of gelato we'll order next. The conversation was stress-free, and when Oliver and I head back in to get gelato, he says, "Sophia is really nice."

"But . . ."

"What do you mean 'but'?" he asks.

"And do you like her?" I replied impatiently.

Oliver seems to deliberate over this for a minute. Jeez. It's not a trick question. But finally, he says yes. He likes her. I advise him to try to hold her hand when we leave. We're heading to the open park, and that's a good place to put his arm around her. I feel like I'm bossing him around, but Oliver has no clue or game whatsoever. He mumbles something that sounds like okay, and we head back outside with the gelato. I notice that Sophia looks at Oliver and smiles big as he hands her the cup of pistachio. He returns it. A smile from Oliver is a big thing these days. I hope that Sophia's smile was for Oliver and not the gelato.

The girls take turns tasting everyone's flavors and decide that the Fondente was the best because it's very chocolatey. Oliver and I gather the trash from the table as the girls start walking to the curb. Their arms are linked, and they're whispering about something but they separate when we get close. Zory automatically moves to me and kisses my check and then locks her arm through mine. Sophia says, "Thank you for the gelato and cappuccino, Oliver," and he just smiles again and nods.

They wander behind us on the narrow sidewalk, so I can't see what's happening. I whispered this to Zory, who turns around and asks, "Are you lovebirds okay back there?" I laugh because she has balls. I would never do that because Oliver would want to kill me.

"Yes, Mom," Sophia answers, and I turn to see her reach down and grab Oliver's hand. I manage to catch a glance of his face and how red it's becoming. I smile and face forward, happy to see my friend blush.

The park in Rittenhouse Square sits in the middle of the neighborhood, and it is, in fact, a square. We walk through one of the entrances and see a small band of musicians playing a rendition of "Tiny Dancer" by Elton John. They're pretty good, and Oliver bends down and puts a few dollars in the open violin case. As he straightens, he automatically reaches for Sophia's hand, and they walk into the park, commenting on the clusters of cute dogs out for walks.

We eventually walk back to the parking garage, and Zory heads right to the front passenger door, ensuring Sophia and Oliver were together for the ride home. Since Sophia was staying at Zory's house tonight, Z's house is our destination. As soon as I park, Z tells me to walk her to her door. I know she wants to give Oliver and Sophia time alone. I don't complain; I want a few minutes alone with her.

When we get to the top of the elaborate steps, I pull her to me and kiss her mouth so hard. She kisses me back just as hard. When we finally take a breath, we both look at the car and see Oliver and Sophia kissing in the backseat. She gives me a small high five just as Sophia and Oliver climb out of the car. I kiss her once more and pass Sophia on the way down. Oliver moves to the front seat as I start the car.

"Soooo, is she a good kisser?" I ask sarcastically.

"Shut up, asshole."

I laugh and tease him, telling him that Zory is going to get all the info anyway.

Oliver is still smiling as I pull in front of his house and say goodbye.

Oliver

I am smiling like an idiot as I unlock my front door. I plan on sending Sophia a funny meme in a few minutes. I haven't been this excited about anything in a long time. I'm thinking about holding her hand. It felt so soft. How does someone have skin so soft?

I'm jolted from my thoughts as I step inside and an ominous feeling takes hold.

It's quiet. Too quiet.

No TV blasting from Mom's room. No sound from the kitchen or basement.

I drop my keys on the entry table and something in my gut tells me to check on Mom.

I walk upstairs to Mom's room. The door is closed, so I knock. No answer. I knock again, louder. Nothing. I open the door a crack and look inside.

Mom is lying face down, like her face is smashed into her pillow. Fear and panic set in before I can even register what I'm seeing. I run to her and turn her over. She looks dead. I easily lift her by the shoulders and start shaking her. I fumble in my pocket for my phone and call my dad.

He doesn't pick up. *What the hell do I do? Do I call 911?*

I lay my mom back down and put my ear to her chest, and I think I can hear her heartbeat, but I don't know if it's her heart or mine.

What do I do? What do I do? What do I do? I panic.

The sound of my phone ringing snaps me out of impending hysteria. It's my dad. I slide the answer bar as fast as my shaking hands will let me.

"Dad! It's Mom. I think she's dead."

"Oliver, are you home?" Dad says, and I hear him moving.

I tell him that yes, I am home, and he tells me to stay put. He's at Kim's and will be there in a second. I don't hang up. I tell him to stay on the phone, and I can hear him fumbling for something, muffled voices, and then I hear a door slam.

I feel like time is standing still. Like I'm watching this whole scene, but I'm not me. I am someone else.

I hear someone at the front door, and I run down and grab the door as Dad drops his keys on the floor and heads up to Mom's room. I'm right behind him. He checks her and screams for someone to call 911. While I'm looking for my phone, I see Kim dialing 911.

Behind her is Deven, who runs up to me and hugs me. Dad leaves the room and comes back not even a minute later with a white and pink box. He hovers over Mom and puts something that looks like nasal spray up her nose. He stands back and waits. I can hear the sirens in the distance but can't remember who called them. Dad checks to see if Mom is breathing. I hadn't noticed the stethoscope in his hand. He inhales deeply, as though he'd been holding his breath this whole time, and says, "She's okay."

There is a crazy amount of confusion as Kim runs down and meets the EMTs. One heads upstairs and the others bring the stretcher and other equipment. I'm just standing next to Mom's bed and tears are falling. I don't remember moving, and I still have that weird out-of-body feeling, watching them load Mom onto a stretcher. Dad tells me that he's riding with Mom and that Kim will take me to the hospital, right behind the ambulance. I tell him that I want to go in the ambulance. I don't trust my dad with Mom. I don't trust anyone. But he tells me that Mom is going to be okay and that he will see me at the hospital.

Kim

I tell both boys to follow me as we hurry back to the house so I can get my keys. I play a quick game of mental ping-pong, trying to decide whether I should leave Deven home with Jules. I determine it will be good for Oliver to have him there, so I ask Siri to call Mom but hung up quickly because I remember that my parents are in Atlantic City. I then call Kana, and she says she'll be right over. I run into the house and tell Julia that Aunt Kana will be coming in fifteen minutes. She's going to stay with her and OP, I explain, and Deven and I are taking Oliver to the hospital because his mom is sick.

Looking confused, Julia asks, "What's wrong with her?" And I tell her that we will talk about it later and to make sure the door is locked behind us and that I will call her as soon as I can. I blow her a kiss and tell her that I love her as I usher the boys to the car.

We arrive at Temple University Hospital and go through the Emergency Department. I go up to the administrator on duty and ask if Aubrey McDaniel is here. She asks if I am a relative, and just as I am saying no, Shawn comes out of the heavy doors that separate the waiting room from the treatment rooms. He walks right up to Oliver, who is pacing, and whispers something to him as he hugs him. He then gathers us all and gestures to the administrator to open the door. He nods and says thank you as he ushers us into a private conference room just inside the heavy doors.

We all take a seat around the table as though we're going to confer about something. And maybe we are, but I would hope that if Aubrey were on life support or something and they needed to make a difficult medical decision, Shawn would have asked Deven and me to leave.

Shawn sits next to Oliver and says, "Your mom is fine. She woke up for a few minutes and is now sleeping. She's on oxygen and should recover."

Tears stream down Oliver's face, and he puts his head on the table in relief.

Shawn reaches over and rubs Oliver's back and gently adds, "But your mom has to make a tough decision now."

Oliver's head jerks up and he snaps, "What decision?"

"Ol, she needs to go to rehab. She needs to get clean. She is destroying herself and hurting you in the process," Shawn answers.

"Wait. What? Why does Mom need rehab?"

I am momentarily shocked by Oliver's ability to completely forget how he has spoken about the possibility of Aubrey having a substance abuse issue.

Shawn holds Oliver's hand and looks him in the eyes. "I know that you think that your mom is sick and maybe she drinks too much, but she is an addict. She has been fighting addiction for years. When you were one, she went to a thirty-day program and did well for a while."

Oliver shakes Shawn's hand off him as if it's contaminated and begins to raise his voice. "You knew that she's an addict for all this time and you didn't get her help? What the fuck, Dad? Did you want her to die? Would that make your life easier, not having to worry about Mom?"

"What? No! Of course not, Ol. I tried to get her into outpatient programs for years, but she refused to go."

"You mean just like you tried to get me a therapist," Oliver retorted.

Deven and I make eye contact. We both feel uncomfortable.

I stand and say, "Deven and I are going to get some drinks for all of us."

Shawn mumbles thanks as we leave the generic room.

　　　　　　　　　　　　　　　　　　　Anna Picari

Once out in the hallway, Deven hugs me and cries. I'm always surprised by how small I feel when I am being hugged by my six-foot, broad-shouldered, beautiful son. But no matter. I am clearly the one doing the comforting and will continue to do so until my last breath.

We stand there for a few minutes and then Deven says, "Let's go find something to drink."

Deven

We get home around one in the morning. Aunt Kana was sleeping on one side of the couch, with OP sleeping on the other. She sits up when she hears us open and close the door. I kiss her goodnight and then kiss Mom and head up to my room.

This night was surreal. It seems like we were at Gran Caffe L'Aquila a week ago, but it was only six hours ago. The cafeteria was semi-open when we went down and got a coffee for Shawn and a Coke for Oliver. We also grabbed a few assorted bags of Herr's chips and brought them up to the conference room. Shawn told us that Oliver had gone to sit with Aubrey.

She is so lucky that Oliver got home when he did. And she was lucky that Shawn was right down the street from the house and that he had Narcan at home in case she ever OD'd. I'm so happy that she'll be alright, but Mom said that she needs to go to rehab and work on getting clean. And that's hard but not impossible. Why wouldn't she want to be healthy for Oliver? He loves her so much.

I texted Zory a few times while we were at the hospital, but it was never in front of Oliver. She told me to call her when I got home, no matter what time it was. But I decide to text her first.

Hey, Z

My phone rings. I say hello and then start to cry. Zory listens as I tell her that I thought Aubrey was dead. I mean, she looked dead. I tell her what a mess Oliver was. I tell her about the fight between Oliver and Dr. McD, and I tell her that I love her. That just slips out, but she says it back: "I love you, too."

Her words swirl around my head and straight into my heart. I wish she were with me so I could hug her. We talk a little more and she finally says, "Go to sleep. You must be exhausted."

"Okay. Goodnight," I say, and I want to add *I love you* but don't just in case the previous I love you was a pity I love you. I mean, you don't not say it back to a person who is crying unless you are a complete and total jackass.

She says, "Goodnight. I love you, Demonio."

I reply, "Te amo, Bronceada."

Zory laughs, and I hang up.

Kim

I bring down a pair of sweatpants and a Ryan Howard T-shirt and hand them to Kana. She's going to stay the night. As she's getting changed, I pull two martini glasses out of the cabinet along with a shaker. I fill the shaker with Kettle One and add a smidge of olive juice. The vodka bottle looks lower than I thought it was, but it's enough for two martinis and I make a mental note to pick up more. I suppose we can switch to wine if need be. I transfer the vodka from the shaker into the martini glasses and garnish with olives. I grab a bag of pretzels and carry them and the two glasses to the coffee table.

Kana comes down with her hair in a ponytail, looking like she did when we were eighteen. The woman does not age. She picks up one of the martinis and then sinks back into the couch, taking a long sip. I do the same and she says, "Spill."

I relay the events of the evening, and she listens attentively.

When I'm done, she says, "So your boyfriend comes with a ton of baggage."

I make a lame joke: "No. She's not more than a hundred pounds."

"Ha, ha. Great deflection."

"I don't know what to say. She lingers in the background of our relationship, but this is the first time that she's caused an issue." I take a deep breath and close my eyes.

"What. Is. Going. On?" Kana asks, enunciating every word.

"I don't know. I have been seriously thinking about ending it with Shawn. I don't think that there's enough to go the distance."

Kana laughs and tells me that I can't break up with him anytime soon because then it looks like I can't handle the addict ex-wife. "You'd look like a C U Next Tuesday."

I take a sip of my drink, which is not supplying the right amount of potency, and tell her that it doesn't matter whether I do it tomorrow or a month from now. Aubrey will always be lurking, and Shawn feels a responsibility toward her because of Oliver. Kana and I just sit in silence for a minute and then I add, "Yeah. I think that I will be easing myself out gradually. Honestly, Shawn should be focused on his son." And I change the topic of conversation, satisfied with my rationale and the plan forming in my brain.

Oliver

I jolt awake as I remember where I am. I check my phone and it says 7:13. Dad is sleeping on a lounge chair on the other side of Mom. I'm in a chair, and I quickly stand to touch Mom's hand. I want to lie next to her, with my head tucked under her arm, like I used to do when I was little. I always felt so safe. She gives the best hugs and makes me feel so special all the time. And now I can't remember the last time I felt that from her. I look at her sleeping in the bed, and she looks like a kid. She's gotten so small, like she shrunk. When did she change? I can't seem to remember because it seems like a long time ago, and it also seems like it was just last week. I don't know.

My nose starts dripping, and I realize I'm crying. There are tissues on that weird half table on wheels, and I take one, swipe the snot, and walk to the window. It's so sunny, and I see people doing whatever the fuck they want. Those people have no idea what's going on here. And they don't care either. They're just walking to get the bus or jogging or whatever, and my life is shit. A lady is pushing a baby in a stroller, and this pisses me off. I mean, I feel like I want to punch something, or maybe I want to punch that asshole lady. She thinks she's such a great mother because she got up early and strapped her kid in and is probably thinking that she deserves a reward. She's probably a shitty mom. And this makes me want to scream, but instead, I walk into the bathroom and cry.

Kim

Kana is awake when I get downstairs in the morning. She's brewing coffee, and I sit down at the counter, watching her. "It's so nice to have someone making coffee for me. Other than an occasional barista at Starbucks, it's always just me." I smile.

"When we retire, let's get a condo in Palm Springs. We can take turns making coffee in the morning."

I chuckle and reply, "Are you planning on ditching your husband?"

"Some days, yes. But retirement will be more fun with you," Kana says as she pours coffee into my favorite mug and fixes it with light cream and a smidge of sugar. The mug is bright orange and has *Kim* written in script in white. She then goes to the cabinet and peruses the olio of mugs. She selects an oversized coffee cup with a rainbow covering it and pours herself a cup. She drinks her coffee black.

Kana plops down on the high stool at the counter next to me, and we quietly sip our coffee. I'm thinking about Aubrey and her next steps. She needs to go to a good rehab. And then a halfway house and then move. Seriously, go somewhere else. In order for an addict to be successful, they need to be away from things that can trigger them such as their favorite bars, a specific food item, and especially people they usually party with.

My mind wanders to Oliver. To say that he was distraught last night would be an understatement. I plan on talking to Shawn again about therapy, and this time, I will force his hand. I can suggest that he calls in front of me. I'll even call one of my recommended therapists' cells for him. I rarely call in favors, so they will answer if they're available. If this fails, I will support Oliver as he makes the call himself. In Pennsylvania, a minor as young as fourteen can seek and obtain mental health services for themselves. I only go this route if the parents are resistant, and Shawn now qualifies as being such. He has one last chance.

My thoughts are interrupted when Kana asks if I'm hungry. I'm not, and I suggest that she head home. We finish our cups, and I get a bag for her clothing from last night. Kana jokes that she's going to keep the Howard shirt, and I tell her to feel free. We hug goodbye. And it's a long hug, the kind that is never awkward because of a long history of hugs. But before she heads out, I ask, "Do you think it's weird that I am twisted and turned inside of Shawn's life so quickly? You know what I mean? Like I'm dating Shawn, helping them out when his ex-wife ODs, and I see Oliver daily."

Kana says, "Yes and no. You are present for anyone who needs help, but the fact that you are romantically involved with Shawn does make it a little weird."

I just nod, hug her once more, and walk her to the door.

As I am rinsing the cups, my phone dings with a text from Shawn.

Hey, K. Thanks for last night

Hey. No problem. How is everything?

Aubrey is awake and with Oliver, who is also awake.

Glad to hear that

We have a meeting with the

Just as I am finishing up the text, Deven enters the kitchen, heads straight to the fridge, and pulls out the milk. He pours himself a glass and chugs and then pours himself a second glass. I walk over and rub his back, and he smiles sadly. "I am worried about Oliver."

"Yeah. Me too."

"Thank God his mom didn't die. I don't know if he could take that."

This statement strikes me because Deven has little memory of his cataclysmal loss. But I wonder if it resides in the darkest recesses of his memory. He was four, and most people retain some memory at that age.

I acknowledge his statement with, "It's never a good time to lose a parent, but you're right. Oliver is a very sensitive kid."

Deven nods his agreement and then rummages through the freezer to find the Eggo waffles. As he waits for his Eggo to toast, he tells me about the big date the night prior, and I can hear happiness when he talks about Zory. I could not have picked a better starter girlfriend for my extraordinary boy. She is a lovely person, and they make a cute pair. Inevitably, one or the other will get their heart broken, but he will always have fond memories of his first love. Deven also tells me that Oliver and Sophia connected, and this delights me. Oliver needs something to go his way. I don't know much about Sophia, but she's not on my radar in any way, so that's a good thing.

Julia

Entry 11

So, I think this may be the longest that I have so far. And why do we have to use the word entry? Like because we are getting into somewhere? That is a bizarro word. Anyway, me and Allie Snapped and Facetimed all last night. My Aunt Kana came to stay with me, and I told her that I was going to bed, but I was awake. Something happened to Oliver, and Mom and Shawn had to leave, and Deven went with them. Mom will tell me what happened later. I was going to go downstairs when I heard her come home. It was really late. Or was it early? I don't know what the right thing to say is. It was 1 o'clock in the morning, so that's morning, right? Do you care? I don't. Anyway, back to Allie. I showed her my thigh. I haven't written about that yet. I wanted to see if Allie was lying about it not hurting, so I used scissors from a mani-pedi set that Gram bought me last Christmas. They are weird-looking, and I don't know how I would use them on my fingers or toes.

I shut my bedroom door after checking to see if Mom and Shawn were still watching television. They watch a lot of TV, and I wish they would go to Shawn's house sometimes. I never get to use the big TV on Friday nights anymore. I pulled up my hot pink Lululemon shorts and just cut my skin. It didn't bleed, but it looked like someone scratched me. It didn't hurt at first because I was thinking about doing it right, but it hurt when I was done. So I think that Allie was telling the truth.

When I showed her, she said that it didn't count because it didn't bleed, but I think it counted. She told me to do it in front of her and called my Facetime. I wanted to say no, but I didn't want her to be mad at me. I moved the camera to be able to see my shorts. And then I did it again and pushed harder. Blood dripped from the corner of the line where I first started. Allie told me to wipe up the blood with toilet paper and flush the paper. I closed Facetime and did that. I started to feel weird about it. Like it is a bad secret. Like a secret that I should tell Mom about. But I can't tell Mom. She will freak out. And I think that she will be really mad at me. I won't tell her because I didn't like this and won't do it again.

Oliver

Dad lets me go with him and Mom when the social worker lady comes to talk to Mom. She doesn't even look like a grown-up. How can she have that job and be so young? Ms. O looks like the right age. This chick looks like she can be in my class. She introduces herself as Bella, and I look at the badges that hang on her lanyard to see if her real name is Isabella. All the girls I know with the name Isabella call themselves that. I think that you need to be really hot to call yourself Bella, and this social worker is not. She's not ugly, but she's not pretty either. She just looks boring as she goes right into the names of a few places that Mom should consider for treatment.

Mom is sitting up tall in a chair, with her wheelchair right behind her, like she's eager or some shit. I feel a little embarrassed for her. Dad sits at the table across from Mom and Bella, and I take a seat in the wheelchair, rolling it to the head of the table. My dad asks a lot of questions, and the social worker responds like she has all the questions and answers memorized. I'm starting to get hungry. Dad got drinks and stale muffins this morning, but I didn't want any of it. Mom ate a chocolate chip muffin like she hadn't eaten in a month.

I remember that Mom may not have really eaten in more than a month just as Bella says to Mom: "Aubrey. It's hard to get clean and stay that way. Remember to remain in the present. Remember your worst day. Remember not to substitute anything for heroin. Not alcohol, not sugar, not even sex."

Heroin? Is Bella saying that . . .? I look at Mom, but she's just staring at Bella with that stupid look on her face, like she's listening to Jesus.

I blurt out, "Mom, you were using heroin?"

She turns to look at me and nods.

I jump up from the shitty wheelchair as I yell, "That's not true!"

Mom stands and moves toward me, and I just push her back into her chair and storm out of the room. I am so fucking pissed that the door is one of those that you can't slam. They refuse to be slammed. They just quietly close. I go back to Mom's room and sit. Heroin is for people who are really addicts who don't have a home and a family. It's for losers who beg in the streets. How could Mom have been using *heroin*? Where do you even get it?

You can get weed in Jersey now, and I think people sell Molly and Adderall at the skatepark. Heroin is found in the shady areas. Heroin.

Suddenly, I feel like a dickhead. Those bruises and bumps. Not leukemia. Fuck. Mom had needles? I am so stupid. I could have helped her if I wasn't so fucking dumb. I am raging at myself. I want to smash my head in the shitty mirror over the sink. I want to punch the wall. I want to scream so loud that the dead rise in the morgue. Then Dad comes in, pushing Mom. If you saw them, you'd think they were still together. He helps her get into bed and touches her hair when she's settled. The nurse comes in to do stuff. My dad puts his arm around my shoulder and leads me out of the room.

"Want to get something to eat?" Dad asks and I say okay.

Dad and I head to Corner Bakery to get food. We order, get our drinks, find a booth, and put our locator, number 15, on the table. While Dad is blabbering about the rehabs, my phone vibrates, and I look down and see a text from Sophia.

Hey

I don't know what to say, and I look at my dad, who is still going on about rehabs like he's going to help me with the answer. Our food arrives, and I take a bite out of my sandwich. Then another bite. Then another bite. I'm only thinking about eating my sandwich when Dad switches gears.

"What did you guys do last night?

I stop mid-bite and say, "Huh?"

Dad repeats the question and then adds, "Didn't you go out with Deven and Zory?"

Before I realize what I'm doing, I respond, "And Sophia."

Dad puts his fork down and looks at me like I just told him I got drafted to the NBA.

"Who's Sophia?"

"A friend of Zory's. She really nice."

In full dad mode: "Is she pretty?"

I want to die. WTF, Dad! Why don't you just ask me if she's hot and puts out? No one uses the word *pretty*, but what I say is something like, "Yeah. She's pretty."

"Are you going out again?"

"I dunno. I'm going to text her later."

"Good plan. Know that I am here if you want to talk."

And I feel angry again. Or you can get me a therapist, asshole. Why would I talk to you?

I would talk to Mom first. I realize that my mom has not been able to give advice or much else, if I am being honest, for over a year, but I want to shout it. I want my dad to know how much it pisses me off that he is playing Father of the Year now. He was never around when I was a kid. He was doing fellowships or in meetings or taking extra calls at the hospital. It was always just me and Mom. What a joke! I'm doing just fine. Thank you, Shawn. But I keep all of this to myself and just nod and finish off the bag of my chips and go to the bathroom. I go straight to a stall and lock the door and lean against it.

Hey, Sophia

Please, please, and then . . .

☺

What does that mean? That's she happy that I texted? That she is just happy? I wish Deven were here to help me. I made the decision to text him.

S sent me a smiley emoji????

what did you write back

NOTHING. I texted you

right
write that you had fun
hanging out

Thx big help

LOL

I go back to Sophia's text and tell her that I had a good time and that the gelato was fire. She wrote back that she wants to go back to try a different flavor. I say something about hanging out again, and she sends a heart emoji. I head back to the table and Dad asks if I am okay. I just say yes and grab my drink to refill. Dad and I go back to say goodbye to Mom, but I don't want to hug her. I'm pissed off at her, but I decided to hug her because she didn't die, and she's here to hug. Dad is already in the hallway, and I turn at the door to look at her, but she is turned the other way, curled on her side. I walk toward Dad and home.

Kim

In the weeks after the incident with Aubrey, things went back to the status quo with me and Shawn, with one exception: we hang out at his house more frequently. Oliver is hanging out with Sophia more, which is amazing. I nonchalantly ask Deven about them, and he seems to answer in the affirmative. One would think that I speak fluent teenage-ese, but I don't. Mostly I interpret body language, and that seems to get me through at work, but reading Deven and now even reading Jules is tricky.

Julia walks around like she has a secret she's dying to tell. But it's a happy secret, I think. I constantly ask if she wants to talk about anything, and she always says either "no" or "not really." I'm going to let it be for now. Julia will tell me when she's ready.

This time of year is hectic for the teachers who are gearing up for finals but more so for the students. They must perform on said tests. I always have an uptick in appointment requests and gladly accommodate everyone. Like I always say, "We are successful when the students are successful." My principal and colleagues believe there are high standards for themselves and the students. The school climate is positive, and that starts with Mandy and ends with the last kindergarten student.

Deven is exempt from all his finals and will most likely be ranked in the top 10 students academically. Like his personality, his brains are from his dad. But he's a worker, too. He busted his butt this year and deserves to be proud. I know I am. He will have an outstanding application to any school he applies to.

We toured Princeton last weekend, and although I've been on the campus numerous times, I appreciated the nuances of the campus that only a tour guide can provide. Additionally, the cacophony of student voices, barking dogs, and bikes rolling by added a picturesqueness. The guides are called Orange Key tour guides. Our guide's name was Kaylee, and she was adorable. Deven is settled one hundred percent on Princeton now. There's nothing more for him to do except continue his community service tutoring. I'm sure he'll like the schools we're scheduled to visit next month, but Deven's top spot will be hard to beat.

After a very busy day and a jampacked week at Freedom, it's finally Friday. Jules and I head home. It's warm out, and the students are permitted to wear khaki shorts with their uniform golf shirts. I notice Julia keeps pulling her shorts down as she gets in the front seat. Are they too small? Is she becoming self-conscious of her legs? I don't want to suggest that she needs a different size because I don't talk about size or weight. So far, Julia is not body conscious, but that can change at any time. I advert my eyes as she pulls the buckle across herself.

Julia is going to Allie's tonight, and Deven is going to the movies with his friends, so I hope that I have time to talk to Shawn. He's been saying the "L-word" more, and I need to be completely transparent. Attempting to curtail our dates backfired. It's as though Shawn needs me more now. Or perhaps he just feels like there's a light at the end of his tunnel with Aubrey safely nestled at Starward Inpatient Rehab Center in Montgomery County.

A feeling of decisiveness comes over me, and pricks of energy course through my veins. I'm ready to tell Shawn that I cannot be in a relationship with him because he needs to focus on his son. Shawn is slowly learning to be a fully engaged father, and he has finally made an appointment for Oliver with Megan Breakwood, LPC. I have known Megan for years and think the world of her. She's the best counselor I know for teenagers. As a favor, Megan added Oliver to an at-capacity client list.

When I think about ending things with Shawn, I feel a heaviness in my chest. It's as if my heart has a tear in it, but I know that he needs to be focused on his home life. I refuse to be in the way of Oliver's mental health. Kids are always the top priority; relationships are secondary.

I ask Deven to drop off Julia at Allie's house on the way to the movies and he reluctantly agrees. Julia is full of energy as she tries to hurry out of the bathroom. I will miss this when Deven goes to college. Hopefully, he'll be close to home so he can visit often. My son won't have a cloying mother whining that she misses him. Private, mental cloying will be my angle as I attempt to pray Deven into visiting as much as possible.

The kids leave, and I hate how quiet the house is. I look down at OP, who is pawing me for attention. He prefers when it's just the two of us, like in his puppy days. If only he had the cognitive capability to understand how dysfunctional that was. I reach down and grab and scratch OP's muzzle. He has been asking for that more and more. He has a vet appointment this week, and I make a mental note to ask about his teeth. I study my old friend for a minute. I love this animal. He's pure joy and seems to understand my moods. I would still be lost without him, and then a sinking feeling comes over me as I calculate his age. Around seventy-five. Seventy-six? Nope. Can't deal with this right now.

I go to the refrigerator and pull out a bottle of Sauvignon blanc. Grateful for the screw top, I pour myself a healthy glass and take a long sip just as the doorbell rings.

I bring my glass and my pup follows me to the front door. I look out of the peephole and see that it's Shawn. *Mental Note: Ring Doorbell.* I open the door, give a quick, one-arm hug, and shut the door behind him. Guiding Shawn to the kitchen while bracing myself for what I have to do, I ask about his day. Friday is surgery day, and he's always exhausted. Instinctively, I pour him a glass of wine and sit near him on the couch.

Shawn talks about one of the surgeries that was particularly difficult while I try to look like I understand the minutiae of the proce-

     Anna Picari

dure. I excuse myself to grab a homemade charcuterie board from the fridge. In the living room, I set down the board on the coffee table, which is a gorgeous light oak table that Matthew and I purchased from an Amish craftsman when we were visiting Lancaster, Pennsylvania. It was a struggle to get home, and we yelled at each while trying to get it in the hatch of my Ford Explorer. Halfway back to the house, it started to rain, and we just started laughing. The experience of getting the table was worth it. It still looks new, and I know that it will be around longer than I will.

Shawn reaches down and takes a cracker, and while he is slathering chili jam on it, a blob of jam lands on my oak table. That must be a universal sign to go.

As I wipe off the table with my cloth napkin, I say quietly, "Shawn, I think we need to go back to the friend zone."

Shawn stops chewing. "What?" he asks while trying to swallow.

"I think we're better off as friends. Being without a partner for so long has made me very independent. I think that you want more than I can give. It's not fair to you." I only half believe what I'm saying but I continue. "I really enjoy your company, but I have so much going on and, more importantly, so do you."

This is a half lie, because other than work, I have very little going on. Maybe I should suggest that we just slow things down a bit. I am feeling resolute in my decision to give Shawn space to focus on family. And watching him leaning forward toward our oak table sucker punches me as Matt flashes in my mind.

Shawn wipes his mouth with his napkin and folds it neatly again, looking for something to do while he gathers his thoughts. He verbalizes all the positive pieces of our relationship, trying to get me to change my mind. I explain all the ways I am ill-equipped to be in a relationship.

Finally, he says, "Okay. I get it. But can we be friends with benefits?"

"What?! No," I say in a firm voice, although I flush thinking about certain benefits.

He starts laughing, and I laugh, too. I tell him that I liked our "benefits," but it's in our best interests to make a clean break.

Shawn, not looking particularly devastated, hung around for about an hour after that, sharing about Oliver's sessions with his therapist and that Aubrey is reporting that she is doing well three weeks into treatment. When he gets up to leave, I walk him to the door. He turns around and gives me a quick peck on the cheek. I return the kiss, and he leaves.

Once I am alone again, I plop down on the couch and OP plops next to me. Reflecting on our time together while unconsciously stroking my pup's soft back, I smile. Shawn was what I needed for those few months, and we will still see one another at games and events, even in the neighborhood. However, I contemplate the real reason that I cut him off: guilt. All of the men I went out with were straightforwardly distractions and were well aware of this about an hour into the date. But Shawn is different, and I am scared out of my mind.

Julia

Entry 12

Yo, yo, Mr. J! Whatzzupp? How is that for a greeting? I like writing these entries because I have so much to say and no one that I can talk to. I think that people at school are jealous of me and Allie. Allie thinks so too. She says that they are jealous of how pretty we are. I don't know about that. Allie is pretty, but I think I am plain. When I say this to her, she tells me that I am blind. That everyone wishes that they had my hair and my eyes. I always thought that my smile was the best thing about my looks. I had braces early, and my smile is straight and big. I may have to have braces again when I am in 9th grade, but I hope not. Mom always makes sure that I have whitening toothpaste, and she makes sure that my teeth are brushed after eating foods that can stain your teeth. Is that weird? I mean, no one talks about how much they brush their teeth and when they brush. But I just do what my mother tells me to because I truly like my smile and want to keep it looking pretty. Allie's mom acts like we are not even in the house. My mom always talks to my friends and has snacks. I don't even know if Allie's mom is home. Maybe she stays in her bedroom. I don't mind. We eat anything we want, and there is always beer in the refrigerator. Beer tastes better than vodka, and I make sure that I have chips to mix with the beer when it's in my mouth. We don't drink every time, but we drank last night. I had two beers and felt very dizzy, and everything was funny. I had to burp a lot, and Allie and I had a burping contest. She won, but it was fun.

Allie asked if I had any new cuts, and I said yes. I pulled down my leggings and showed her my hips. She looked proud of me or something. I felt bad. I would never be proud of this, but I like the way that I feel when I do it. It's like there is no time or anyone near me, and I don't have to think about anything else except the scissors. It feels like the scissors are doing all the work, and I am just watching. It's weird. Allie then shows me her arms. I am surprised by the cuts that are on her arms. They are at the top of her arms and they are really red, like they are angry or something. I think that I made a sound when Allie pulled up her sleeve because she said "what" in a not-nice voice. I told her that the cuts looked like they hurt, and she said that they didn't and pulled her sleeves down. She then got up and went and put on a hoodie. I didn't mean to hurt her feelings. I was just worried that she was hurt. I tried to tell her that but she got mad and said that she wasn't hurt. We watched YouTube videos for a while, and then my mom came for me. It was 10 o'clock.

Anna Picari

Kim

OP loves a car ride and wags like a crazy dog when I ask, "Do you want to take a ride in the car?" I think he knows the word *car*, but honestly I could be saying, "Do you want to get a drink in a bar?" in a singsong voice and he would behave the same way as he charges to the front door. It's beyond cute, and it makes me happy. OP runs to the backseat door, and I open it. He sits on the back driver's side like he is waiting for me to seatbelt him, but he's not. He's waiting for the kiss that I always plant on his head when he first gets into the car. It started when he was a puppy and I was struggling to be comfortable in a car. His jubilation at getting to ride swelled my heart, and the only way I could convey my love for him was by kissing his head, so it became a ritual that has lasted almost thirteen years.

It's not yet July, otherwise known as the month of death, and I am well aware that I will be tethered to my dog for the month. My grief and sense that I may have inadvertently caused Matthew's death by asking him to go and get Deven and bring him to the hospital sometimes still comes to mind. I knew that he'd had limited sleep the night before. *Why did I ask him to drive?* I frequently ask myself.

Shaking my head, I know that I cannot play the "what-if" game right now, so I decide to block out the date until the last possible moment. This will leave me little time to consider Julia's birthday, but I have managed to get it done for the last several years. The first few years after Matt's death, my mom took care of it and hit a homerun every time. My parents and Kana made sure that holidays and birthdays happened, and I will be forever grateful. Julia's first birthday was a blur for me, but there are a ton of pictures showing Julia laughing and brutishly grabbing and smashing a pink piece of cake.

I'm glad I brought OP with me for the twenty-minute ride to Allie's house in South Philly. It's nice to have company. Driving through the neighborhood, I think about Matthew's family. His mother was/is a tremendous cook. My favorite meal was her homemade gnocchi with braciole, and I feel a stab in my heart as I again realize that my children may never know her or the extended family. To this day, the month pulls me into an abyss of grief and regret. I hate July . . . but I love Julia.

I shake the feeling of sadness and regret out of my mind as I park in front of Allie's house. I really would like to meet her mom, but OP will have a doggie panic attack if I get out and leave him, so the in-person introductions will have to take place another time. I have spoken to her on the phone once, and she sounded reasonable enough, but the call lasted only two minutes. Legit face time is required so that I can get a sense of who she is. The decision is made to invite her into the house next time she drops off her daughter. I park in front of her condo and text Julia.

Hey, Jules. I am here.

A few minutes go by. I text again.

I'm here. With an excited OP.

K

It takes about five additional minutes for Julia to come down. She sits in the backseat with the dog. I wonder why she doesn't sit in the front but don't ask. Sometimes dealing with a preteen is like trying

Anna Picari

to maneuver a skittish, rabid raccoon out of your trash bin. I ask her if she's okay. She says that she just wants to sit with OP, but I am incredulous. Julia loves riding up front because she controls the music. She incessantly attaches her phone to my Bluetooth, so Taylor Swift or Lizzo is usually playing in the background when we talk.

Letting it go, I pull away from the curb. "So," I begin. "What did you guys do?"

"You know. We just hung out."

"Could you be more specific?" I ask gently.

"Jeez, Mom! We didn't do anything." Julia sounds defensive.

I peer over my right shoulder at a red light and see Julia looking at OP, stroking his back.

"I didn't say that you were doing anything. I was making conversation, Jules."

Julia relaxes and says that she is really tired and rests her head back and closes her eyes. Understood. She doesn't want to talk anymore. I drive in silence and worry about what exactly she's not saying.

Julia struggles with maintaining friendships. I used to watch her at classmates' birthday parties, which were held at various bouncy house places or bowling alleys, as she just followed the group and always sat at the end of the long tables, talking to no one.

We arrive home and OP leads the way to the front door, not without peeing on the arborvitae near the stairs. I open the front door, and he runs in and immediately goes to his spot on the couch. Sometimes, I call him "Sheldon" in reference to the idiosyncratic protagonist from the sitcom *The Big Bang Theory*, because he curls up on the same spot on the couch and will nudge you with his nose if you sit there. Julia heads straight up to her room, and then I hear the shower running. I wonder why she has to take a shower but let it go as I settle on the couch, next to "Sheldon" and click on the television.

Julia

Entry 13

So Mr. Jablonofsky, my final entry. Memorial Day was last weekend, and I know that you will be walking around to check to make sure we did this assignment. Before I forget, I want you to know that I liked writing my thoughts down. I think you should always make your students do this even though everyone complained about it. I did not know that I had so many thoughts. If it's okay, I am going to keep writing to you. Someone gave me a diary for my last birthday, and I will keep writing in that. It's not an old-fashioned diary, with a key and all, but it's a pretty notebook with GIRLS RULE on the front cover. I have not written anything in it yet and I hope that I remember where I put it because that birthday was almost a year ago. Anyway, this notebook is just a plain ugly black and white notebook. I hope I get an A on this. You told us that we only had to do 10-15 entries and this is number 13, which I think is a lucky number. I like getting A's on things. It's weird because I feel so proud and that I am better than everyone else. Is that wrong? Mom tells us to be humble (I know what that means) because it's nicer not to brag. I try to be nice to everyone, but lately, some people are being mean to me. Talia Shapiro asked me why I am friends with Allie and said that she is weird. I don't think that she is weird. I think that she is funny. I don't think I like Talia anymore. I liked her before. Talia is really funny though, and we have fun in the humanities program. Do you know what that is? You probably do, but I'll explain it anyway, just in case you don't know. Humanities is for smart kids. My mom told me that all the kids take a test in 2nd grade, and the smart kids get to take a special class. Tbh, I want to stop going next year, but I am afraid to tell my mom. It's fun and all, but I want to hang out with Allie more, and I think the humanities class messes up my schedule. Allie says that I should mess up in that class on purpose so that they will throw me out, but I don't want to do that.

Maybe I will ask my mom during the summer. She is not as busy but she is always in a weird mood in July. Sometimes we go to Disney in the summer. Mom has PDs there and sometimes she is a presenter. That sounds like someone who gives out presents. You know what that means. LOL. Do you have to go to PDs too? Mom says that they are usually helpful, but some of them are dumb. What do you think? I don't know if Mom is going to be a speaker this year or not. Once me and Deven got to sit in the seats and listen as Mom talked about helping children who have behavior issues. It was boring, but everyone looked like they were listening. I played on my phone for the whole time. Deven too.

Look! I made a new paragraph. Sorry that I did not do that a lot, but no one will see this, right? Just checking again. Because I am cutting myself a little more than I was before. I even made a pattern. It looks like a #. I think that's funny because I think of funny hashtags when I cut. #blood #weirdscissors Stuff like that. I told Allie about this, and she laughed. She thinks I'm funny. Allie wants me to go to her house all the time. It's fun, but sometimes I am scared. Her mom is not home a lot, and there is a lot of noise. I don't tell her that I am scared sometimes, but I want to be at my house more. Mom or Deven are there, but no one bugs us. I think Mom wants to bug us, but she doesn't. I tell her some things that we do but not everything. She would freak out for sure.

I hope you have a great summer. You are a nice teacher, and I hope I get you again next year.

Deven

Zory. Don't need to say more. I cannot believe that she is mine. After I got back from the movies with the guys, I Facetimed her. I was texting her during the previews, and Oliver nudged me and made a "what the fuck" face, so I stopped. I used to be pissed off at guys who always had to be in contact with their girlfriends. But I get it now.

I want there to be an invisible rope connecting us at all times, or really, I want there to be an actual rope keeping us tethered together. Like she can live her life but also be secretly tethered to me. Does this sound creepy? I know that's not going to happen, and I worry that she's applying to schools that aren't on my list. And what if she goes out of state? She's applying to the University of Florida because her family has a house there. Who wants to live in Florida? It's basically a swamp.

I would give up the dream of being a Tiger to go wherever she goes. I think her top choice is Penn State. I'm pretty sure I'll get in there, but I don't really love that school. Honestly, there's so much hype around it that I didn't think it lived up to. Everywhere we walked, there were students yelling "We are!" and then the people on the tours answered with "Penn State." And it was kind of cultish, as if they'd already drank the Kool-Aid. And it's in the middle of nowhere. I guess I am just a city guy. I don't see why anyone would choose to live anywhere else but a city. The best thing about it was the campus creamery. That ice cream is fire.

After our college tours were done, Mom was all "college this, college that." It's not even July, and she's bugging me to start on my college essays. Not only that, she wants me to write about my dad's death. I don't know if this is some technique to get me to talk about Dad's death or if she wants me to go for the drama. I barely remember anything about it. Plus, she's talking about hiring a private college counselor. She insists that it will help me get into Princeton. I don't argue. She's going to do what she wants to do. And I think she needs a project to get past July 25. It sucks for Julia, and I don't know if she notices the change in Mom around this time of year, but we all pretend to be happy for her. Gram and Pop will come over, and we'll have a cake. Julia always picks a cannoli cake from Altomonte's. It's really good, but I always pick the limoncello cake for my birthday.

My brain moves to its favorite pastime: Zory. The thought of Zory going to college without me makes me want to throw up. She claims that I can be possessive, but I don't see it. Well, that's not entirely true. Last month, I saw her laughing in the hall with Theo Kumar. I am basically a pretty chill guy, but I wanted to push him into the wall and start punching his face. I didn't, but believe me, Theo looked like a Picasso painting in my mental rendition of what happened.

Instead, I walked over and said, "What's so funny?" Zory looked confused at first like she was wondering why I was there.

Theo answered, though, which pissed me off. "We totally fucked up our chem lab, and Ms. Moore looked at what we were doing and just shook her head. It was hilarious."

My face must've conveyed that I didn't think he was funny, so Z added, "You had to have been there." I nodded and put my arm around Zory's shoulder. It may have been my imagination, but I think I felt her body get stiff. But Theo took the hint and said goodbye.

I don't want any other person making Zory laugh. That's my job.

We get along most times, but lately, we've been arguing. I want to have sex. Not just blow jobs or hand jobs. Actual fuck-action. I'm getting tired of being a virgin. No one knows this except Z because I have a reputation to uphold. I try to act modest, but I know that there are a lot of girls who are interested. Not to brag, but I am smart, athletic, and kinda good looking, and I can easily get laid, but it should be more than that. My first time, I mean.

I don't think Oliver is a virgin anymore. Sophia and Oliver have been together since the end of basketball season. It seems codependent, and he almost backed out of our college tour because he didn't want to be away from Sophia, but he seems happy for the first time in a year. I'm happy for him. He's a good dude. The four of us are heading to the shore next weekend, thanks to Zory's parents. They booked us two rooms at a not-so-nice hotel that's near the boardwalk but at least the rooms are connected so I hope that it's Z and me, Oliver and Sophia.

I call Oliver to confirm plans, and he asks about the sleeping arrangements. "Am I sleeping with you? Please say no." I just laugh and say it's up to the girls.

Oliver

I've never met anyone like Sophia. She is *real*, you know? And she really cares about me and my life. She knows all my shit and loves me anyway. She wants to be a psychologist, and I think that she would be good at that. I told my therapist about that, and she said that Sophia sounded like she would be perfect at that job. My therapist's name is Megan. She is nice and has a really big smile. She really listened to me after Mom's overdose.

Soph and I were just hanging out after school in the stairwell behind the cafeteria and she asked me if I was okay. "Yeah. I guess," I said. And she sat closer to me and held my hand.

"I'm here if you wanna talk," Sophia said. But I didn't want to, so I just put my head on her shoulder and we sat in silence for a long time.

It's been a few months since then, and I can actually say the word *addict* now, but it still pisses me off. Megan says that I'm holding on to a lot of anger about Mom's drug problem and that I was in denial because I didn't want it to be true. She may be right, or maybe my mom is just sneaky, I think. Megan says that I have Major Depressive Disorder. She pulled out a list of symptoms, and I checked all the boxes. Here's how this goes:

Megan: How's your appetite?

Me: Sucks. How's yours?

Megan: Oliver, stop deflecting.

Me: You stop deflecting.

Megan: What do you mean when you just said that your appetite "sucks"?

Me: Do you need synonyms for "sucks"? Okay. Let's see. It means bad. It means that it's the worst. It means I never feel hungry. I only want to drink soda and eat potato chips.

Megan: Thank you for answering my question.

This goes on for a while and then . . . surprise! Megan the Super Therapist thinks I should be on medication. I don't want to take antidepressants, I argue, but she says that it's best to do talk therapy along with pharmaceuticals if warranted. She actually uses that word, and I try not to scream. Megan wants me to talk to my dad about it since he's a doctor and all. But he's an ENT. I don't have a sore throat. I promise Megan that I will talk to him about it before my next appointment, which is in two weeks. I see her every other week, but I had to skip the last session because we were touring Pitt and Penn State.

I liked both of those schools. Pitt is smaller but pretty. It looks like a college you would see in the movies. But it sure as fuck didn't make me change my mind about Penn State. Sophia is applying there, too. That would be perfect if we went together. We could go to have dinner together and have sex all the time. I really like sex. Everyone talked it up all the time, and I gotta say, it lived up to the hype. But I don't know if I did it okay.

Sophia had sex once with Henry Thompson last year at someone's graduation party. He is heading to Duke next month, so I don't have to worry about Sophia seeing him at Penn State. I'm glad he's not at the school anymore so I don't have to see him. I used to think about his dick and if it was different than mine. Mine is a normal size, according to the internet, and I hope that's true. No one ever explained how to have sex, but I think I figured it out. It was like I was hungry and needed to taste every part of Sophia. She tastes like salt and honey. The first time, I just did what my body told my brain. Unfortunately, my brain should have told my body to hold off jacking because it happened too fast. I was too excited to be embarrassed about it, but I wanted to die in

Anna Picari

shame later that night. I try to slow down the jacking now.

It's really like my brain talking to my dick: "Don't blow yet. List the Eagles players in the Hall of Fame. Don't finish now." And it usually works. But I only get to Brian Dawkins or Reggie White. She seems like she's having a good time, if you know what I mean. Harold Carmichael. And I finish before I can add another player.

Deven says that I need to watch porn but it weirds me out like I am a creeper or something. Cave people didn't need online porn, and neither do I.

Dad is holding off putting the house on the market until next school year. He says that he wants me to have a stress-free senior year. I try to convince him not to sell at all. I like our house, and Mom will always need a place to stay. I don't say this out loud. Dad would freak. I think that he's happy that Mom is working part time at a hair salon answering phones and then going back to the halfway house. It sounds fancy, but it's not. It's an old house in Northeast Philly, and Mom has a roommate because there are only four bedrooms. When I visit, Mom says that she likes the women living with her. She feels supported. I try to ask her about what's going to happen after the halfway house, but she always says she's living minute by minute. I get that. Ms. O used to talk about mindful living when I used to talk to her. She's nice, but I'm glad that Megan does not know my teachers and friends and has never fucked my dad.

Kim

Shawn. In the Whole Foods prepared food section. He's talking to the pizza maker and then, just as he's placing his order, he looks up and sees me. He gives a wave, then the one-finger *wait* signal. I nod and walk his way. He hugs me, and I inhale his scent, Eros. He's wearing scrubs, and damn, he looks sexy. I pull away and he asks if I can stay and have a bite to eat with him. I look in my cart—broccolini, yams, Pirate's Booty, case of Topo Chico. Great, nothing that needs refrigeration—and then say yes.

At the Whole Foods seating area, Shawn talks about how happy Oliver seems. He briefly touches on Aubrey, but I know that he thinks that's why I ended it with him. It's not, really. It was mostly about my feeling disloyal to Matt. So I told myself that it was just about my need for sex. Shawn woke my sex up, and he was a wonderful reentry into the world of orgasms, sans battery-operated items, but he wanted more. I'm not convinced that I will ever be able to have an emotional relationship with a man.

I still mourn for my husband and the family that we had just fucking started. Matthew was my great love, and no one should have to settle for being number two. These fears were addressed long ago in therapy, and I am very aware of my inability to accept anyone else's love. This is why I have been thinking about creating a Tinder account. My greatest issue with this is that it may figuratively kill me. I may actually die of embarrassment if any of my coworkers or parents saw me online, so that's probably not going to happen.

Time passes easily as we eat the pizza slices we ordered, and Shawn asks me if I want to go get a drink. I know that I should say no, but the twinge between my legs says yes. I tell him that I will meet him at Gingers in about an hour.

I hurry home and put my groceries away, take the stairs two at a time, and hustle to take a quick shower, just in case. Then I freeze, and the memory of being told that Matthew had passed overwhelms me. I remember it as if it were yesterday: I was sitting up in the hospital bed, holding a sleeping Julia in my arms. I remember looking down and thinking that she was beautiful and that our family was now complete. A nurse came in, and I was going to ask her to help me take a shower, but then I noticed two police officers step into my room behind her. All the air in the room seemed to have been sucked out of it, and I instinctively pulled Julia into my chest tighter. The very young officer told me that Matthew had been killed in an automobile accident. I remember hearing the words but having no idea what they meant. I felt Julia roll out of my arms and I think I asked someone to get her. I must have just stared at the officer because the nurse squeezed my hand and asked if she wanted me to put Julia in her bassinet. I must have nodded. The next thing I remember was my mom lying next to me in the hospital bed, cuddling me as if I were a child.

As I shake myself out of my misery, I pick up my phone to call and cancel my meeting with Shawn. But then I put the phone down. I take a cleansing breath, look at my reflection in the bathroom mirror, and change my mind. And although the memory is imprinted into every molecule of my body, I still struggle with reconciling the fact that my family is incomplete.

***

I get to the bar a few minutes late, and Shawn is already sitting in a small booth, sipping on what I believe is scotch, a welcoming martini set across from it. "Hey. Sorry I'm late."

"No problem. Drinks arrived a second ago," Shawn says as he lifts his glass. I pick up mine and clink his, deliberately avoiding eye contact.

We fall into easy conversation and have a few laughs. Fuck. Shawn is such good company, but I cannot see myself sharing all of me with him. I have too many scars.

We ordered another drink, but I was already feeling tipsy. The bartender makes oversized martinis. After we finished the second drink and a plate of nachos, Shawn asks if I want him to drive me home.

"Maybe you can drive to your house," I say suggestively and, most likely, drunkenly. He leads me to his Tesla and opens the passenger door. Jazz floats out from the surround sound speakers, but we are silent. The silence continues until we are in his living room, where he grabs me and pulls me to him.

We start kissing, and our tongues are circling as we taste one another's familiar flavors. We kick off our shoes and move to the couch. Shawn grabs my breasts with both hands. He pulls my shirt out of my shorts and over my head and slides his hands under my bra. I gasp as he finds my nipples and pinches. There's a fire between my legs as I fumble for the string of his scrubs. I untie them and stand, pushing him back onto the couch.

Grabbing the waistband of his underwear, I yank both the underwear and the scrubs down and pull them over his feet. I open his legs and lower my head until I'm able to put him in my mouth. He lets out a loud sigh and relaxes his head onto the sofa as I stroke his cock. After a minute, he lifts me up and says, "I don't want to finish yet." Message received as he moves me to the couch. He unsnaps my bra and licks my nipples until they are soldier-erect. Before I realize what he's doing, my shorts are off, and his mouth finds my clit, and I'm ready to scream. I grind myself against his face and let out a slew of unladylike words. He grabs hold of my arm and pulls us both down onto the plush carpet, and I land on top of him. Shawn was just as prepared for this as I was, I realize, as a condom appears from seemingly nowhere just in time for me to straddle him. He comes fiercely, and I shakily say, "I guess we *are* friends with benefits."

Part III

July–September

Julia

Girls Rule #1

Hello again, Mr. J!! I can't think of a way to start this book, so I am using your name. I liked writing my feelings down, so I am going to keep writing in the notebook that says GIRLS RULE on the cover, but I like being able to tell someone about them. It's July now, and I was starting to miss you. LOL. Thanks for the A in your class. I had all A's, but I got a B in Science. It is so boring.

I have been busy this summer. Gram and Pops took me to the shore for a week and Mom came down for the weekend. It was fun and boring. I missed Allie. I love Gram and Pops, but they don't like to go on rides. Pops goes on with me anyway, and he looked like he was going to throw up after we got off of the Extreme Cyclone. I asked Mom if Allie could come. She said that she would think about it, but she finally said no.

Allie and I spend all our time together when we are not doing "family stuff." Mom jampacks things to do into the summer because "family bonding time is very important." It's okay. I don't mind. We always go to Hershey Park and the shore. Sometimes we go to Orlando so Mom can go to a conference. But this year, we are not doing that. When we go to the beach this summer, I will have to wear my one-piece swimsuit because it comes down lower on my hips, and I don't want anyone to see my hashtags.

One night, Allie was sleeping over my house and wanted to go into the kitchen after Mom and Deven went to bed. I had a bad feeling that she wanted to drink vodka. I said okay, and we went downstairs. I got two glasses from the cabinet and hurried to the fridge to get the lemonade out. Allie said, "Good idea. We can pour the vodka in that so it looks like we are just drinking lemonade." I wanted to tell her that I did not want vodka. I didn't want to hide anything else. The bottle made a weird sound like a gulp as Allie poured vodka in our lemonade. I was mad, but I didn't tell her that I was mad. I put the vodka away and got a bag of pretzels. We each took our glasses upstairs. After we were in my room, I tasted my drink. The vodka tasted better with lemonade. My anger went away as we scrolled through IG and TikTok until we fell asleep. But when I woke up, I felt bad again. Allie was still asleep, so I went to the bathroom. I locked the door and searched in the back of the cabinet for my scissors. I grabbed a washcloth as I took my shorts off and looked for a spot to cut. My hips have all kinds of lines now. Some are light, and some are dark. But I always cut in the shape of a hashtag because it helps me focus. I wet the washcloth because I knew that I was going to have to clean up blood. The first cut always hurts, but then it doesn't. Top to bottom. Top to bottom. Side to side. Side to side. Hashtag was done and I wiped it with the wet washcloth. I held it there for a few minutes to make sure the bleeding stopped. I rinsed out the washcloth and put it in the hamper.

I feel better now that I told you. TTYL

    Anna Picari

Oliver

Sophia has been weird since we got back from the shore. I know that I fucked up, and I haven't heard from her since we've been back. I text her, but she doesn't respond. When I ask Z about it, she tells me to give her time. But I can't lose her! I just can't!

One night when we were at the shore and were sitting around a small table, Deven had gotten hold of a bottle of rum and a six-pack of beer. We mixed the rum with Diet Coke and ice from the machine that was right outside our door. We were all kinda drunk when Zory suggested we play Truth or Dare. We were laughing and having a ball until it was Sophia's turn. Zory asked her, "Truth or Dare?"

Sophia answered, "Truth," probably since the dares involved us removing a piece of clothing or having to sing the "Bob the Builder" song off the balcony. Some things like that.

Zory asked her, "How many penises have you touched in your lifetime?"

Sophia got quiet like she was thinking about it.

I jumped up and shouted, "Two. You only touched two!"

Sophia laughed and told me to sit back down. Then she dropped a bombshell. "That's not right, Oliver."

I stood again. "Two. Me and that other douchebag. One. Two."

"I only had *sex* with you two," she said with a little laugh as she got up and faced me.

"You're kidding."

Sophia just laughed as if that was an answer, so I got in her face. "Tell me you're kidding!"

She kept laughing, so I pushed her. Not hard or anything, but since she was drunk, she fell and hit her head on one of the chairs. Blood appeared out of nowhere, and we were frantic. I ran to the bathroom and got some clean hand towels. Z grabbed one from me as Deven filled one with ice and put it on her head.

Zory said that we should go to the hospital or an urgent care. Sophia kept repeating that she was fine but started to cry. She kept saying that she didn't want to get arrested for underage drinking. I looked at Deven, and then Zory looked at Deven, and she looked *pissed*.

Finally, Zory sat next to Sophia on the bed and smoothed her hair. She gently moved Sophia's hand, which was covering the cut. "The bleeding has really slowed down, Soph," Zory said kindly. Sophia sniffled as she walked over to the mirror. The cut, which looked like it was a little more than an inch, was above her right eyebrow, closer to her hairline.

I stood behind her and wrapped my arms around her, but she broke through my arms and told me to get off. I felt like someone had just punched me in the gut.

"I'm going to crash with Sophia tonight," Zory said, and Sophia muttered something like a thank you. They both stood and walked to the adjoining room, but not before Zory grabbed the half full bottle of rum and slammed the door.

As soon as they were out of the room, Deven's glare landed on me. "What the fuck, Ol? What the hell was that all about?"

I didn't know how to answer him. I had no idea what just happened other than I'd hurt Sophia. I know that I sometimes turn into a huge dick when I'm drunk, but I don't go around pushing people. Deven looked so mad, and I remember sitting on the edge of the bed and putting my head in my hands and crying. I grabbed my hair like I was trying to pull it out. Deven sat down next to me and put his hand on my shoulder.

"What did I do? Oh my God, Deven. Fucking-A! I hurt her! I love her so much, and I fucking hurt her!" I said between my sobs.

I still can't believe it. I hurt the person who cares for me more than anyone in this world. She is the person that I would give my life for.

In that moment, I stood up and started slapping myself. And I couldn't stop. Deven yelled for me to stop and tried to grab my hands. He ultimately won. He's bigger and stronger than I am. And I'm bigger and stronger than Sophia. I started to cry again.

Deven

Lying in my comfy bed at my house after that whole Oliver/Sophia thing, I start thinking about Oliver. I hope he tells his therapist about the incident, but I bet he doesn't. He was mortified. And I'm glad. What the hell was he thinking? You never lay hands on anyone, especially someone smaller than you. Then I began to worry that Sophia's going to break up with Oliver, and that would not be good. I know they probably won't get married or anything, but he'll go totally off the deep end if they break up. He seemed happy and then goes and does something so idiotic to fuck it up. I text Z.

awake?

yes

how is Soph??

What do you think??

is she going to break up with Oliver

Idk 💔

you know

I don't think she is thinking

OK. r u ok

Yeah guess so

I love you. Ur a good friend 🖤

I love you too. xo

goodnight Dev

goodnight Z

I want her to call or Facetime me. When she doesn't suggest it or do it automatically, I let it go. I feel like I am somehow responsible for Oliver's behavior. It happened so fast, and I don't believe that he meant to hurt her, but Jesus, there was a lot of blood. I told Zory that Oliver's personality changes drastically when he drinks, so she knew that I knew. That's why she looked at me to do something, and I froze. So maybe she's right to blame me. He's like two different people. It's fucking frightening. He walks around school looking like he's itching to waffle someone, and when we hang out, he is practically mute. It's so bad that I try to limit the hard stuff when he's hanging out with our group. The guys know how he gets and tell me not to include him when we're gaming or whatever. He would be wrecked if he knew this, but he gets argumentative. To say that he turns into the biggest dick would be an understatement.

I briefly contemplate talking to Mom about this. She's so good at handling other people's problems but gets kooky when I have a problem. When I was in third grade, a kid would always look at my tests. I told Mom and she said to try to cover my work. So, I used my left arm to make a shield around my test. The kid started poking my arm with his pencil until I moved it. I told Mom about this, and she got mad. I still don't know why she was mad, but as a little kid, I remember being really confused. Was she mad at the kid for poking me? Was she mad at me for being a baby about it? Was she mad at the teacher?

And then there was the time when something weird was happening with my balls. I think that I was about twelve or thirteen. One of them was bigger, and they both hurt. I was embarrassed to talk to Mom, so I lived with the pain until, finally, I fell off my chair while we were eating dinner. The pain was so bad that Mom rushed me to the hospital. When the doctor told Mom that I needed surgery, she started to cry. I told her that I didn't need surgery and that I was feeling much better. Later, Mom explained that I felt better because of pain medicine. I'm glad that Gram came to the hospital to be with us while Pops watched Jules. I think Mom freaks out because of what happened to Dad.

But this is not about me, it's about Oliver, so maybe she won't be freaked out. Decision made, I close my eyes, and next thing I know, it's morning.

Kim

Deven comes downstairs earlier than usual on a late July morning. It's ten thirty, but he looks like he hasn't slept a wink. He goes immediately to the coffeemaker and lets out a grunt when he sees I've already cleaned it. I tell him to sit down for a second while I make another pot. "Everything okay?" I ask nonchalantly as my gut instinctively knows that it's not.

"I dunno. Something weird happened at the shore," Deven says as I bring cream and sugar over to where he's sitting.

"What do you mean 'weird'? Like someone flashed you outside Manco & Manco's or like something weird happened with one of you?" I question as I pour Deven coffee into his Eagles mug.

"Oliver."

Deven says it like it's a complete sentence, and it may as well have been. There's a weight to the name that says it all. I immediately go into social worker mode and take the stool next to him.

"What happened, honey?"

Deven sounds clinical as he relays the story of Oliver getting drunk and pushing Sophia. He goes on to tell me that Oliver changes when he drinks, and not in a good way. I find the entire story alarming, from the drinking to the push to the slapping himself. I put my arms around my son and squeeze him and murmur that I'm glad he told me.

"You can't tell Shawn." Deven jumps up.

"Why not? He's his parent. I would want to know if it were you."

Deven goes on to explain that I don't understand. That Oliver trusts him and that he doesn't want him to think that he's been betrayed. Deven's voice cracks as he says that last part, so I concede. "How about this? I'll talk to Oliver next time I see him and then decide."

"Are you asking me if it's okay, or just finding a way to tell me that you're going to do what you want to do anyway?"

I kiss his forehead. "You know me so well."

Just as Deven is heading up the stairs, I ask if he ever drove while drunk. Deven says that he hasn't. That his crew wouldn't do that. After my son takes his coffee upstairs, I just sit with thoughts of Oliver. Does he get drunk every time he drinks? I'm well aware that high school students drink, but it's unnerving to hear that Oliver's personality shifts that much. I hope Deven invites him to come over soon; I don't want to have to wait until the school year starts. I take a breath and push this conversation out of my mind.

I'm having dinner with Shawn tonight and don't want to blurt out my concerns about Oliver. As a partner in a relationship, I should share the information about Oliver with his dad. As a licensed mental health provider, I feel a duty to address it with Oliver first. He is seventeen, not seven. This is one of the challenges of my job and probably why Mandy warned me about dating a parent. That said, I wish I had not started this whole thing with Shawn because I'm starting to have *feelings* for him.

Ugh. I don't know what I want. He's a good guy, and he clearly loves me. But even after all these years, I'm afraid to get involved with a man. I'm secretly grateful that, up to this point, the dates were disastrous. Kana says that I should just let things happen organically, but I have things to consider, and I certainly do not want to lead Shawn on if I'm not ready. Will I ever be ready to let a man back into my life, a life that I have carefully carved for myself and my kids? Deven will be at college soon, but what about Jules? It's always been just the three of us. The Three Musketeers, the Three Amigos, the Three Stooges. A few months ago, I truly felt that it was over with Shawn, and now? Now, I seriously don't know. I've missed Shawn, and that scares me.

Julia

Girls Rule #2

I have soooooo much to tell you, Mr. J. First of all, I had my first kiss last weekend. Allie invited some kids over. Some of them were from school like Josie, Aditi, Cate, Liam K., Sailor, Liam B., and Josiah. And some of them went to different schools. The kids from different schools looked older than the kids from my school, but they seemed nice. There was a lot of beer there. When I asked Allie about it, she told me that some of it was her mom's and some came from her friends. Liam K. started telling everyone that we were going to play Spin the Bottle. I heard of that game, but I didn't know anyone that played it. We moved a table and sat in a big circle on the floor. Allie said the rules. One of the rules is that we had to kiss whoever it pointed to. I didn't want to have to kiss a girl for my first kiss. I like girls, but not in that way. When it was my turn, I wished that the bottle landed on Josiah, but it didn't. It landed on Liam B. We both crawled to the center of the circle and kissed on the lips. His lips were really dry, and he smelled like beer, but it was okay. We both laughed after we kissed and then sat down. One of the girls from the other school got me. She is really pretty, but she only kissed my cheek. I can't remember her name, but I am pretty sure that it was an old-fashioned name. But I liked kissing Liam B. I never thought about him like that. I looked at him more that night and decided that he was cute. And I am pretty sure that I saw him looking at me, too. Allie's mom, whose name is Sidney (she told me to call her that), came home before everyone left. She said hi and then went into her room. Kim would have freaked out. LOL. I would have been on lockdown for months or years.

I slept over Allie's that night and we talked. Allie thinks that she likes boys AND girls, but I only like boys in that way. Sometimes I think Allie *likes me* likes me. She looks at me funny sometimes, and once, when we were sleeping, she held my hand. I wasn't really asleep, and she wasn't either. I just let her hold my hand and pretended to be asleep. It was weird, but it was nice at the same time.

My mom picked me up at 11 in the morning the next day. I was waiting for her to text me to come out, but then I heard the doorbell ring. Allie went and looked through the peephole and said, "It's your mom." I looked around the room that was still messy from the night before, but we threw out all the beer cans. My stomach was starting to hurt as Allie opened the door. "Hey, Ms. O," she said in a fake voice.

"Good morning, Allie. Is your mom available for a minute?" Allie looked super nervous, and she looked at me. I didn't know what to do.

Allie said that she would go and get her and headed upstairs to her mother's room. I tried to distract my mom by talking, but that was an epic fail. My mom was looking around at the living room. It was a mess. There were bags of chips and pretzels everywhere and the furniture was in weird spots. Allie and her mom came down. Sidney's hair was in a messy ponytail, and her makeup was all smudgy. But she seemed ok. She said something like, "Hi, there. Kim, right?"

My mom nodded her head and put her hand out for a shake, and for a second, Sidney hesitated. It was a weird thing for my mom to do. They weren't at a business meeting. My mom is so embarrassing. Mom said something like, "It's great to finally meet you in person. You see my daughter more than I do some weekends."

Sidney laughed at that and said, "I really like having Julia here. She is a great kid." I remember that perfectly because I am the greatest kid. Allie looked at me with a weird look as her mom asked my mom if she wanted some coffee. My mom said that would be great. I knew she would.

                                                Anna Picari

Kim

Jules and I drive home in silence, which I appreciate because I have to get my thoughts together. I have been leaving my daughter at the home of someone who primarily works in the evenings. So, basically, they're left unattended. I get that they're in seventh grade now, but to be left alone as often as they are is inexcusable. And by the way the kitchen and living room looked, they hosted a party last night. Unsteady on her feet, Sidney appeared like she was still drunk. There's no way she finished her bartending shift and came straight home. She was a mess. Her hand trembled slightly as she poured the coffee, and I thought about asking if she needed help, but I didn't want to offend her. Sometimes I annoy myself when I think that I need to tell others how they should best live their lives. I need some time to decide how I will handle this with Jules.

I pull into my parking spot, wondering who my daughter is. Julia has been spending time with a girl who throws parties. What the hell? My emotions ranged from anger to sadness to feelings of incompetence. The familiar feeling of the hole in my life that Matthew occupied threatens to deplete me. This is so unfair. I should have her father with me to navigate this with. Guilt rushes over me like a tidal wave as I feel like I singlehandedly screwed up my child.

The car door slamming interferes with my guilt and grief. Jules cannot get out of the car fast enough and almost catches her backpack in the car door. I hear OP barking at the door and look up to see Deven open the door for his sister. His eyes move questioningly to mine through the windshield, and I hold up one finger. He caught my message and closes the door behind Julia. I put my head on the steering wheel and take a deep breath. I don't want to tell Julia that she can't be friends with Allie anymore, but something will have to change. First off, no more sleepovers at Allie's house. Or maybe all hangouts must be at our house. I can make sure that either Deven or I are home. The question looming large in my mind as I get out of the car is this: am I still able to trust Julia?

OP greets me as he always does: like he hasn't seen me in a long time. I squat down and scratch his face, which is turning whiter by the day. I cannot think about OP getting old right now. Or ever. I head to the kitchen and pour water from the fridge. I drink it quickly and then refill it. I set the glass on the counter and text Kana. She immediately calls me, and I head to the basement for privacy. Rehashing the story from the pickup makes me nauseated. Naturally, she advised me to talk to my daughter. Of course. But I share that it is going to be difficult to pretend that I approve of her friendship with Allie. As soon as I say it, I feel like a hypocrite. A judgy, self-serving hypocrite. I want my daughter to have friends but am I going to limit exactly who that friend is just so that I can sleep better at night?

Kana and I chat for about twenty minutes, and then I go upstairs with a plan. I'll wait a while before I bring my concerns up to Jules. I need her to lower her defenses first.

Anna Picari

Julia

Girls Rule #3

This is the first time that I wrote twice in one day. But I have to get this out. I am really upset. Mom told me that I could not spend the night at Allie's anymore. She asked if we had a party last night. I told her that it wasn't really a party. It was just a group of friends hanging out. She asked who was there, and I told her the names of the kids from our school. I don't know why I kept the other kids out of it, but I just figured that it would get me into more trouble. She asked me if we were drinking. I lied. I feel so bad about this. I try to be honest, but I really don't want to be grounded, and I really don't want Mom to tell me that I can't be friends with Allie!

And something weird is happening to me. The whole time Mom was talking, I kept thinking about cutting. I thought of the hashtags that I would say to myself as I cut. #liarliarpantsonfire #beerisbad #kissingliam #twofaced I thought that I did it to impress Allie or because I thought it was cool like I had a secret. But today, I want to cut because I am so mad at myself. I used to think that I was a good person, but I am not.

Deven

I know something happened with Mom and Julia last week, but I really don't want to get in the middle of it. Is that wrong? I'm supposed to be on Julia's side all the time, but I have my own shit going on. There are major negative vibes when they're together. Mealtimes are torture. It's like we're strangers eating together. They are so alike, it's weird.

I cannot wait for school to start, that's for sure. Summer vacation started great but went in the toilet fast. And besides, I really want to submit my applications. My Princeton app is complete, and I just have to submit it. I'm applying Early Action (which is Princeton's name for getting an acceptance earlier) so the admissions people know that it's my top choice, but I need to wait to make sure that my teacher recommendations are ready to go. And I won't bug a teacher in the summer.

Zory and I hang out a lot. We try to avoid talking about Oliver and Sophia, which is hard because they're our friends. Things are going okay. We say "I love you" to each other a lot, but I know that I more than love her.

Last night we were just at her house watching dumb YouTube videos and kissing in between. There's no word in the English dictionary that means how much I feel for her. She said that she's thinking about doing it. I asked her if she knew when, but she didn't. She will know "when the time is right." To make it special, details are essential. It's a big event in a person's life, and people remember the specifics about their first time, don't they? I won't forget it, that's for sure.

We go to her house when her parents are out. And they go out a lot. Not that they bother us when they're home. Zory's bedroom is nice. It's twice the size of my room, and she has her own bathroom. It's perfect for a first time because she has a king-sized bed with a thick and comfy beige comforter. We used to hook up on the small couch in her room but not anymore. I'm getting a boner just thinking about the bed and Zory.

My plan is to get wine from the basement for the occasion. We have a lot of wine stored there. I don't know about other people, but I've been thinking about it since I was eleven. That's when Mom told me about it. Like I said earlier, Mom talks about everything. Sometimes, I wish she was a little more uncomfortable with some topics. She ends these conversations with something like, "Please, please, please come to me with any questions." But I never do because it's less awkward to ask Google. I'm so afraid that I won't do it right. From the videos I've seen, it doesn't look too hard. And the girls always look like they're having a good time. But they're actors, so who knows? I just need Zory to give me the word and I will do whatever she wants.

Oliver

I can't stand it anymore. I text Sophia and ask her if we could meet up somewhere. It's more like begging, but I don't care. I need to find out if we're over, and I need to see her face. I can't eat. I am sleeping like shit. I cannot stop thinking about her.

Hey, Soph

Come on. Come on. Come on. Answer me. Vomit is coming up. I have to swallow it down. I take a four-count breath like Megan showed me. It helps sometimes, but my stomach is in knots. *Please. Please. Please. Please. Answer me.* Finally!

Hey

can we meet?

. . .

. . .

I don't know, Ol

please
I need to see you

fine
you can come here

When

maybe next weekend

k

I may be babysitting.
I'll let you know

let me know. I love you

me too

She didn't say I love you back, but she did say "me too." And that means something. I feel so much better. But that doesn't last.

She finally texts me and says that I can come over on Sunday afternoon. Like a fucking idiot, I ask her if her parents are going to be home. She texts back: "Yes. I do not want to be alone with you." I am such an asshole. Does she think I would hurt her again? I would never, ever do anything to hurt her ever again. But I'll do whatever it takes for her to feel okay with me. I owe her that.

It took forever to get to the weekend. But Sunday came. I took a long shower and gelled my hair. It's kind of long now, and I usually put it in a man-bun.

I can't decide whether to pull it back or keep it down. I keep it down. The day drags on until I can finally leave to go to her house. I have been using Mom's car because she has no use for it and says that it is a "trigger." It's a Toyota Camry in metallic blue and is nice, except for a few cigarette burns on the driver's seat. I get to Sophia's house exactly at 2:00 p.m. Her dad answers the door and doesn't say anything. He only nods at me when I say hello. My heart drops into my stomach.

This is not good.

Sophia comes down the stairs and tells me that we can go to the basement. I walk down the steep stairs behind her, and we sit on the couch. Not next to one another. I'm on one end, and she's on the other. She isn't even sitting on the couch; her butt is resting on the edge of the sofa. We just look at each other. I feel like I need to speak first.

"Thanks for letting me come over."

"It's okay." Sophia looks down at her feet. "I decided that I can't be with you anymore."

I can't say anything because I feel tears coming. I'm not some asshole who would manipulate her with crying. Am I? I need her. The tears come. Words don't.

"Say something," she says, looking at me.

I can't talk. If I speak, I will start bawling. I can't breathe. This is what it must feel like to suffocate to death. I don't realize that my nose is running until I taste something salty on my lips. I wipe it with my sleeve.

Sophia moves next to me and takes my hand. "Please say something."

I just shake my head. There's nothing I can say.

I stand and walk up the steps and out the front door.

You know when you're driving and you arrive at your destination and have no idea how you got there? That's what happened to me on the drive home. I kept thinking of what she looked like when she said that she couldn't be with me. Her face was so sad, but I knew she wouldn't change her mind. And I can't blame her. I don't deserve her. I don't deserve anything good.

***

The following weekend is Labor Day. The fucking official end of the mother fucking worst summer of my fucking life, and it could not come and go faster. Dad had this brilliant idea to go to the shore for Labor Day weekend. He has a buddy who has a condo on the beach.

 Anna Picari

We went. I pretended to have fun, but I kept thinking about the last time I was at the shore.

One afternoon, we sat on the balcony looking at everyone putting up umbrellas and slapping sunscreen on their kids. Dad made comments about all the people just lying there baking. I grunted my part of the conversion. I was not really listening because I was wondering if I would land on someone walking by if I hurled myself over the balcony rail. We were on the eighteenth floor.

Things like this have been on my mind lately. Like, I'll be driving on I-95 and wonder if I'd die if I rammed my car into the back of the tractor trailer in front of me. Or if I have the balls to jam one of the fancy knives on the kitchen counter into my heart. Am I strong enough to push it through my chest?

On the way home from the shore, I think about jumping off the Ben Franklin Bridge. There's a sidewalk, but it's very popular, except in the winter. Who wants to walk on a bridge in 23-degree weather? Plus, I would have to be able to lunge forward like an Olympic athlete because the Patco train has tracks outside the walkway. The Walt Whitman doesn't have a walkway, but then I'd have to drive. I wonder if it's possible to drive off that bridge. Otherwise, I would just have to park the car in the left lane, get out, and jump. With my luck, someone would mow me over with their car, and I'd survive but be a quadriplegic or something. But if I were in a wheelchair, I wouldn't be hurting anyone. Maybe that's what I deserve.

I promised Megan that I would tell her if I was having dark thoughts, so I should probably tell her about these. I've had them before. Before, I was focused on ways to buy a gun. Dad is anti-gun, but he does have a taser. I'm not sure if you can taser yourself into nonexistence, but it would probably be weird. Like, I don't want to be spazzing on the floor or anything. You have to be twenty-one to buy a handgun in Pennsylvania but only eighteen to buy a shotgun. I don't plan on hunting myself, so I'm not interested.

Ironically, I am riding shotgun with my dad, who has zero clue what's going on in my head, as I text Megan.

hey, Megan

Oliver, you ok?

Yeah
thinking about 1000 ways
to die. LOL

Are you committed to anything?

nah. just thinking.

You are coming on Tuesday?

4:30?

see you then

I'm still texting when Dad asks if I want to stop and get food. I say okay. The diner has a great turkey club with fries. As Dad pulls into the parking lot, I start to feel guilty about lying to Megan.

Anna Picari

Julia

Girls Rule #4

Mr. J., I think my mom may be right about Allie. I mean, she never came out and said that she is not a good choice for a friend, but I know that she thinks it. My mom lets her come over and even sleep over. And because we start school on Tuesday, Allie came over last night for a sleepover. It's five in the morning now, but I can't sleep. Allie brought these gummies that were shaped like triangles with sugar all over them. She took one and a half and handed me the other half. I put it in my mouth and started to chew. It tasted so bad. I spit it out into my hand. She got mad and told me to eat it. I asked her what it was, and she just kept asking me if I didn't trust her. TBH, I trust her less than before. After I swallowed it, Allie told me that it was weed. And perfectly safe. I didn't believe her. I started to cry and she said that I was being a baby and that it's legal in New Jersey and it wouldn't be legal if it was dangerous or anything. That is probably the truth, right? Do you ever do weed, Mr. J? I bet you don't because you always have organic chips on your desk. We would always talk about taking some of the chips when you weren't looking. And you look healthy, and you have that pretty wife and little boy. Sometimes, during class, I would look at the picture of them and imagine you being a great dad. That little boy is lucky to have a dad, especially you. I can tell that you really like kids. Your little boy won't do weed gummies.

I didn't like what happened to me. It felt like someone took my brain. Like my brain was actually missing. And then I started laughing at how dumb that was, and I couldn't stop laughing. I laughed so hard that I thought I would pee my pants. We must have been making a lot of noise because my mom peeked in and asked if we were having fun. We both thought that was hysterical, and Mom just gave a wave and shut the door.

But it's not funny now.

Deven

I am sound asleep when Jules comes in hysterical. But it isn't loud hysteria. It's quiet. She's crying and whispering to me to help her. It takes a minute for me to realize that I'm not dreaming. I roll over and sit up fast.

"What's wrong, Jules?" I shout in a whisper. "Are you okay?"

I turn on the lamp that's on my night table. All I see is blood.

What the hell is happening?

It takes my brain time to comprehend what I'm seeing. Julia is covered in blood. I cannot describe exactly what went through my head, but I'll tell you this: I thought Julia had been attacked with a knife or shot or something.

Before I realize what I'm doing, I'm screaming "Mom! Mom!" at the top of my lungs.

Mom appears in what seems like both a second and an hour. She immediately turns on the ceiling light, and I will never forget how wide and petrified her eyes are. Running right to Julia, Mom asks, "Did someone do this to you?"

I guess she was making sure that we didn't have an intruder or something. OP is old and deaf. He's not much of a watchdog.

"No," Jules replies. "I did it."

As she's speaking, Mom's taking the top sheets off my bed and wiping Julia all over to see where the blood is coming from. Julia looks like she's in shock or something as she lays down sideways in the middle of my bed. Mom is focused on her right thigh. There is a long gash that's bleeding fast.

Mom holds a bunched-up wad of sheets on the wound and says, "Deven, go and get some washcloths with cold water on them. Jules, breathe with me," and she starts taking deep breaths with her.

When I get back to the room, Mom and Julia are in a world of their own, and the bleeding looks like it stopped. I can't take my eyes off all the cuts on Julia's legs that appeared as soon as Mom wiped the blood away. Mom has tears in her eyes and Julia is crying again. I want to cry, too. Jesus. What the hell happened to my sister!

The crying slowly becomes different now. Mom lays down on the bed next to Julia and wraps her arms around her. I lay down on the other side and do the same thing. All three of us cry together as Mom and I hold Jules tight.

Kim

I only partially notice that the time on the oven says 6:15. It feels like I've been awake for hours or maybe days. I make coffee on autopilot and pour myself a cup. I sit at the counter and just stare down into my coffee cup. There is no cream. There is no sugar.

Julia must have been cutting herself and dropped the scissors on her foot. This is why we couldn't determine where the blood was coming from. But the reality is this: My daughter self-injures. I begin to cry again. And the urge to throw my coffee cup across the room overwhelms me.

I am so angry: at Jules, at myself, and at Matthew. I put my head in my hands and close my eyes and think, *I am so fucking mad at you, Matt. You should be here, helping me. Is your death somehow connected to Julia's slicing herself like a tomato? What the actual fuck?* Tears are coming faster now as I open my eyes. I still cannot see. I feel more alone than I have in a decade.

I continue the mental self-flagellation. My baby is in pain, and I had no idea. I am a horrible mother. I have imposter syndrome. I ask myself: Am I so self-centered that I didn't notice?

Julia showered in my bathroom, and I gave her a T-shirt to wear. I didn't want her to wake Allie. I put Neosporin on her fresh cuts and bandages on several of the ones that I thought could start bleeding again and then tucked her into my bed. She fell asleep within minutes, and I kissed her beautiful head as I silently closed the door behind me and then came downstairs.

Deven hugs me from behind, bringing me back to the present. I reach back and squeeze his strong arms and say, "There's coffee." Deven pours himself a cup and sits next to me in silence. I don't know what to say to him. He must be freaked out. I know I am. Finally, "I am so proud of you and happy that Julia trusts you."

Deven gives me a small, slightly cynical smile and says, "I love that pain in the ass." He waits a few minutes and then asks, "What now?"

"Since tomorrow is a holiday, I'll call someone who specializes in self-injurious behavior on Tuesday." I did not add that I would be doing body checks until she is well immersed in treatment or turns twenty-five, whichever comes first or both.

"Yeah," Deven responds absentmindedly. Then adds, "I think it's Allie's fault. Julia has not been the same since they started hanging out." He then went on to tell me about the first time Allie was at our house and about the vodka and the vomiting. A wave of numbness overcomes me, and then anger, and then resolution as Deven apologizes profusely for not telling me. He explains that he wanted Julia to feel like he was a confidant.

I understand, but I don't understand, if that makes any sense. Deven should have told me his feelings about Allie without being specific. I would have done things differently, like impose the "only at our house" rule from the start. And then I start to laugh sardonically, because at our house, children get to drink top-shelf vodka and slice themselves like tomatoes. But I also know from years of experience that sometimes kids do exactly what they want to do, no matter what security measures are in place.

After inundating Deven with numerous questions, I feel like I can handle the situation. "Allie could be a negative influence, but it's not her fault," I say while continuously thinking that it's entirely *my* fault.

Deven wants to know why anyone would intentionally *carve* themselves. I cringe at his use of the word *carve* but explained that individuals who self-harm are looking for a release, a distraction, or control.

I go on, "It's not a sign that someone wants to kill themself, although that unfortunately can happen." We finish our coffee in silence, and I head up to my room.

Julia is not there. I quickly go to her room, tap once on the door, and open. Allie and Julia are sitting on her bed, facing one another talking. Startled, they both look up and they both look scared. Firmly, I say to the two of them, "I want the two of you to get dressed and meet me downstairs in ten minutes." They both nod, and I leave the room.

I am on the couch with the latest Lisa Scottoline book in my hand, not reading a word, when Julia and Allie come down. I look at Allie and ask, "Did Julia tell you what happened this morning?"

She simply nods, suddenly looking very young and a little scared.

I respond with a nod and then continue. "Allie, I will be driving you home today. And at that time, I will be speaking with your mom."

Allie opens her mouth to say something, and I just hold up my hand.

"There is no discussion on this. She needs to know. This is a big deal, Allie. I need to know that you are safe and that an adult in your life can take charge of this."

I squeeze her hand and then grab Julia's hand, letting them both know that I am on their side. They squeeze my hands back in a weird unison, and then I ask, "Who wants chocolate chip pancakes?"

After I finish cleaning up breakfast, I text Shawn.

GM

GM 🩶
Listen, I have to cancel tonight

Everything ok?

Yeah. Jules is going through something

Want to talk about it?

*It's fine. I just want to hang here
with the kids tonight.*

Understood. Tomorrow?

*Can I let you know? It's the first day
of school for staff, and I may be
physically and mentally wrecked.
😁 Education is a job for people
in their 20s 😬*

Gotcha. I <3 U

I <3 U too. Talk to you soon

I have Allie text her mom to see if she will be home when we are getting ready to leave. Once Sidney's presence at home is confirmed, I tell Julia that she has to stay home with Deven. She starts to protest and then wisely thinks better of it, calls OP to come down from his current perch on the top of the stairs, turns on the television, and snuggles with the dog.

Sidney meets us at the door, looking somewhat put together. It's noticeable because she was really messy the only other time we met. She shares a nervous smile as she waves her daughter and me in. The house is in much better condition than the last time I was here, and for some reason, I feel comforted by this fact. Sidney asks if I want something to drink and I politely decline. I ask if we can speak privately, and Allie immediately takes the hint and heads to another room.

"Is something wrong?" Sidney asks as soon as Allie is out of earshot.

"Unfortunately, yes," I say and then share that Allie is self-harming. I leave out our family drama from the morning. She can ask her daughter about specifics later if she wants to know how I found out. I also offer to send her the names of local therapists who specialize in dialec-

Anna Picari

tical behavior therapy and work primarily with adolescents. Sidney is gracious but does not appear surprised. I stop myself from asking her if she knew that Allie cut because I don't want to know the answer. We make insignificant chitchat about the upcoming school year and then I head home, looking forward to my kids, my dog, pizza, and a few episodes of *Stranger Things*.

Oliver

September is really busy for most seniors but not so much for me. I did what was required, like writing essays for college applications so that my English teacher could edit and grade them, and I started on applications. I don't even know if I want to go to college, so I'm not in any hurry to fill in anything. I only have one class with Sophia, and that is Psychology, which has about thirty-five students, so I make sure I sit way in the back. Sophia is a front-of-the-class kind of student. I still feel like throwing up when I think about not being with her. It's been about a month since we broke up, and I can't get it out of my head. That night plays over and over in my mind. I talk to Megan every week, and I have been taking Zoloft, which is supposed to help with depression and anxiety. I don't think that it's working because I still feel sad and worried all the fucking time.

And I still feel that blinding white anger, like I want to punch someone's face for no reason. Megan told me that Zoloft can take up to a month to work and made me promise that I would not stop taking it. I promised, but I didn't mean it. I deserve to feel shitty. I am a shitty person, and the world will be better without my sorry ass. I shared this last thing with her, and she made me sign a suicide contract. Yeah. Okay. If I'm dead, you can't take me to court for not living up to my end of the contract. HA! She also forced me to call my dad and tell him how I felt and then chimed in with, "Oliver, tell your dad about the contract." I am red-hot pissed, but I managed to say that I just signed a piece of paper that says that I wouldn't off myself. Jesus! *Way to have my back, Megan.*

Part IV

October–December

Julia

Girls Rule #5

Hey, Mr. J. It's been a lonnnnnnggggg time. But my therapist Kristy wants me to talk about everything, instead of writing things down. I have to add things that I want to talk about to this app she had me put on my phone. But I miss getting things off my chest right away. You'd be proud of me. I have not cut for a long time. Allie is not doing it either. She goes to counseling, too, but not with Kristy. You'd like Kristy. She is very tall. How tall are you? Kristy may be as tall as you are. Anyway, she is really funny and understands me. We talked a lot about my dad and how I feel about it. I don't know for sure, but sometimes I feel that it's my fault that he died. Like if I hadn't been born, then he would never have been in a car accident. But if I was never born, you would never know me and that would be a big loss for you. LOL. School is good, and I am sad that I don't have you this year. I always want to stop by your room and say thanks to you, but that would be weird because you don't even know what I am thanking you for. Well, I will tell you. You were my friend, and I told you my secrets. But don't be mad because I don't see you as much. I have Kristy, my mom, and Allie. You would not even recognize Allie. She cut her hair, and her mom let her get highlights. She looks pretty and not so angry. She used to look mad all the time.

Thanksgiving is next week, and I wanted to make sure that I told you that I am grateful for you. It should be fun. My mom loves Thanksgiving and we are having a lot of people over. OP will be so fat by the time it's over. So TTYL!

Kim

September and October blow by, and the school year is in full swing. October is filled with pumpkin-carving contests, parties, and standardized testing. And there is always a prodigious amount of pumpkin-scented and pumpkin-flavored things at every turn. Not to be a hater, but Pumpkin Spice Lattes are disgusting. They taste like drinking a watered-down cup of coffee out of a Spiced Pumpkin–scented Yankee candle. I know this is not a popular opinion, but I stand by it.

And although Halloween can be a grief-trigger time for me because of Matthew's weird fascination with the holiday—he liked to go to Halloween parties and our house always was the stand-out in our neighborhood—I made a vow several years back to appreciate the joy that children have anticipating the holiday. I make a point of asking any child that crosses my path, "What are you going to be for Halloween?" The explanations make my heart happy. Children love to talk about their costumes. I quickly learned that sometimes a child would ask, "What are *you* being for Halloween, Ms. O?" So I tell a tall tale or two to make the children happy. I think of costumes that would be interesting to the students. And FYI, this year, my fictitious costumes (depending on the age group inquiring) are either Skye from Paw Patrol or Hermione Granger from Harry Potter, both positive female role models, even though one is a fictitious, animated dog and the other is a witch.

November is my favorite month because the leaves are orange and yellow, and the air is crisp, bordering on cold. Snuggling up with Shawn weather. Sweater weather. Social worker's weather, if you will. And Thanksgiving is my favorite holiday because I have much to be grateful for. Deven turned in his Early Admission application to Princeton. Julia has been in therapy with a fantastic DBT therapist named Kristy. She submits to regular checks and has not cut since the summer. My parents are healthy, and OP was just at the vet, who said that he looks fantastic for a senior dog. But this year, the thing that I am most grateful for is Shawn. We have gotten so close that we sometimes talk of moving in together even though we haven't been together for a year yet. Obviously, we would wait until Deven and Oliver leave for college. The only issue is that I don't want to leave my house. Is that wrong?

It's just that Matthew is everywhere in the house. He refinished the baseboard and crown moldings as well as the floor. He added discrete recessed lighting and updated the bathrooms. More importantly, it's the only home that Deven and Julia have ever known. This is where I want them to bring their spouses and their kids. Shawn appreciates the architecture of my house and knows that I have a strong connection to it, so who knows? For now, it's a wait-and-see thing. Besides, my kitchen and dining room are the best for having a big holiday sit-down dinner, and Thanksgiving is one hundred percent my thing. This year, I will be hosting ten people, not including me and the kids. Obviously, my parents will come. Mom and I work well together in the kitchen and, traditionally, sip Cabernet all morning.

This year, I included Shawn, Oliver, and Aubrey. Yes, I included my boyfriend's ex-wife. She is working hard to make amends to Oliver, and I truly appreciate her efforts. Kana and her husband, Dave, are coming with their two daughters—Alexis and Cameron—and Cameron's girlfriend, Madison. It's sure to be a fun day. The Macy's Thanksgiving Parade will be on the big screen in the living room until it's football time.

And like I've said, I am very appreciative of my relationship with Shawn, who, while kind and funny, appears to have been getting better looking as of late. Not to sound like a forty-something cliche, but I cannot believe that I have found love again. We have fallen into a comfortable rhythm and get along so well. And the sex? Well, he has actually managed to teach me a thing or two, which I didn't fathom was possible.

This past weekend, Shawn suggested that we head to an apple festival in Lahaska. He took me to a hotel instead. Once inside our suite, I saw that there was vodka on ice (with sliced lemons), a charcuterie board, and a pair of handcuffs on the table. Shawn poured vodka for both of us and squeezed a lemon into mine. He then took the lemon and ran it all over my lips as he tipped the vodka glass into my mouth. I was ready to go, but he made me drink the entire glass, and then he downed his glass. He roughly kissed me, tasting like vodka and lemon as he started to undress me. I tried to undress him, but he grabbed my hands and held them in one of his big hands as he continued until I was in nothing but my panties. The next thing I knew, my hands were cuffed to the iron headboard, and he was rubbing lemon on my nipples and tasting them, one at a time. It drove me into an ecstatic frenzy. He took ownership of every crevice of my body, and I willingly let him. This was unequivocally the hottest sex that I have ever had, evidenced by the fact that my legs were wobbly when I finally got out of the bed, and my vagina was sore for two days after.

But today, on this crisp Monday afternoon, as I'm finishing my lunch at my desk, Mandy pops in and sits on my couch. I wipe my mouth and stand. "Do I need to close the door for this?" I ask. Usually when Mandy comes to my room, it's something she wants to discuss privately, out of sight of the office staff. They are very discreet, but I swear they know all of our secrets—staff and students.

"No," Mandy answers.

"Okaaay," I reply, feeling incommodious.

"I continue to be concerned about Oliver McDaniel," she says straightforwardly. I open my mouth to say something, and she just

                                        Anna Picari

holds up a hand and says, "Hear me out."

I nod and sit down on the couch, one cushion away from her.

Mandy starts, "His grades are slipping, worse than before. And he is listless."

I sit there for a minute, looking at her. So many thoughts are racing through my mind. I'm frustrated because I check in with Oliver almost daily and notice every nuance of his demeanor, actions, and words. "I appreciate your concern. I promise I will make sure that he's okay."

Mandy scoots closer to where I'm sitting, takes my hand, and squeezes. I squeeze back and say thank you. And just like that, she's back in principal mode. "I have to head to the cafeteria now. There's a rumor that the freshman students are planning a food fight."

I give a little laugh as she heads out my door.

I close the door and pull down the shades on the two windows on the wall behind the couch. I turn on the small lamp on my desk and turn off the overhead lights. I kick off my shoes and sit on the floor, my legs crossed "crisscross applesauce," as the kids say, with my back resting against the back of the couch. I begin breathing and repeat my mantra "toooooo," which is my abbreviated form of the word *intuition*. I meditate to facilitate more accurate perceptions and thoughtful discernment. This helps me in my personal and professional life, but I have a sinking feeling as I attempt to move further into my meditative practice today that it is somehow failing me. If what's going on with Oliver and Julia are indicators, I am probably correct about this.

Deven

At school, some of the guys were teasing me that I always get what I want. We just got a quiz back and they noticed my grade, along with the correct bonus question. A guy in the class said, "You are such a *dick*. How did you get that bonus right? It was impossible."

I just shrugged and mumbled that I didn't know, but then a guy named Thunder Hale turned and said, "Orsetti lives in the land of perfection." I almost replied that if I did live in such a place, no one with a douchebag name like his would be there, too. But I just kept my mouth shut and glared.

I know that everyone looks at me and thinks I have everything. I have a beautiful girlfriend, a ton of friends. I'm good at basketball and people generally like me. I have no idea why, though. Mom says that it's because I have Dad's personality. For my entire life, I have been hearing about how perfect Matthew Pasquale Orsetti is. Mom said that Dad had "a smile that would light up a room," and that made his eyes crinkle. He was charismatic. I don't think I am, but Mom says that I have an innate ability to draw others to me while making them feel good about themselves. This is total bullshit. I am overly nice to people because then there's a smaller chance for them to see me for what I am . . . a fraud. And apparently, my dad was a highly intelligent guy who had a degree in electrical engineering. Is this why I want to be an engineer, too? Have I been receiving subliminal messages that I should follow in his dead footsteps? *I am so fucking lame.* Obviously, my mom was nuts about him. But was he really that perfect? I mean, he died so young that maybe he didn't have a chance to let his dick-ness out. Maybe he cheated his way through college. Maybe he wasn't so goddamn perfect.

This feeling of fraud has been overwhelming me lately. I'm sure that the admissions officers at Princeton are going to see right through my bullshit. I have no energy to participate in my classes and I recently learned that, apparently, I am a failure as "a man."

Zory finally greenlighted sex. Her parents were heading out of town for the weekend, and we would have the house to ourselves. I told her that I would pick up food and bring it over. I went to Mario's and got a couple of takeout platters and fried calamari. Z loves calamari. I stopped at the ACME and got a big bouquet of flowers, which the salesperson specially wrapped. There was a big purple ribbon. I borrowed a bottle of wine from Mom, without her knowledge obviously. And I was ready. At least, I thought that I was ready.

I drove to Zory's house with a knot in my stomach. I tried to figure out why I was stressing. We'd done pretty much everything except it, and we always had fun. But I was grateful for the bottle that was rolling around on the floor of the backseat. I found a spot on her street and gathered everything from the car. She must have been looking for me because she was waiting on her front steps. I walked faster to greet her, and she came down the stairs to meet me. I handed her the flowers and we kissed. We kissed longer than is probably appropriate in a neighborhood with young children. I didn't care who saw or what anyone thought. I love Zory so much that I want to be permanently joined to her all the time. I asked her once if we could always share our locations, and she flipped out. I backpedaled real fast and told her I was only joking, but I wasn't. I think she knew that I wasn't joking, but she let it go—one more reason to love that girl.

Once inside the house, Zory put the flowers in a vase and put the vase on the kitchen table. Her kitchen has a table that's like a corner booth in a diner. It's really cool, actually. It's shaped like a circle so that we can sit next to each other. We're not weirdos who sit next to each other when we're at a restaurant, but it's hype that we get to do it at her house. Zory transferred the food onto real plates, and I opened the wine. I picked one with a screw cap on purpose. The last thing I wanted to do was to fuck up a cork, which my mom does frequently. Z had wine glasses out, and I poured the wine. I know that you don't fill wine up to the top of a glass like beer, so I filled the glasses three quarters of the way to the top. Zory sat down in the center of the booth. I put the glasses down on the table so that I could slide in. She raised her glass, and then I raised mine. "To us," she said as we clinked.

We ate most of the food and drank most of the wine. I was feeling buzzed, and I could tell that she was too. I remember thinking I should've nabbed two bottles because that knot in my stomach was still there. Zory stood up, finished her glass, and said, "Let's go to my room." I swallowed the remainder of my wine and followed her. I have been in her room more times than I can count but the door had always been open. That's her parent's rule, and I don't want to piss off her parents. But that night, I closed the door behind me.

Zory pulled off her turquoise-colored leggings and turned to me. She grabbed my hand and led me to her king-sized bed. Sitting on the edge as she knelt in front of me and unzipped my pants, I suddenly felt like an intruder and I wasn't sure why.

She pulled my jeans down and over my feet. I had kicked off my sneakers as soon as she started to unbutton my pants, and I gave myself props for being proactive in the shoe department. I just wanted her to take my pants off asap. I noticed that the nervousness left once nature took hold.

Zory told me to lay back on the bed, and I moved up, closer to the headboard. She crawled up between my legs and sat there with her legs tucked under herself. We kissed until my lips felt numb, and I was *ecstatic*. But at that moment, nature failed me. I flipped her onto her back, praying to any and all gods to help me get hard so that I could finish this. But I didn't, and I couldn't.

Deven

Basketball tryouts were hot. We had a lot of new faces and some good talent. I don't have a say in who makes the team, but I know who I would choose. I don't think Oliver will make it, and it sucks because he's a senior. But the dude is not putting any effort into it. He stares into space instead of listening to the coaches, like he's too important to learn something new. I elbow him or step on his foot when I can, but the coaches are noticing. I'm going to put a good word in for him, but it probably won't help him. Oliver is so moody lately that he makes me seem like *I* am all even keeled. And that is not true . . . because I seem calm on the outside, but I'm not.

Things with Zory have been weird since I couldn't finish. I googled "Reasons an eighteen-year-old can't ejaculate" and "why can't a teenage male maintain an erection." I don't think there is anything physically wrong with me because I jack off all the time. Lately, though, I'm afraid to do it because I know I'll freak out if I can't get hard.

I have no one to talk to about this uncomfortable sex stuff. If I tried to talk to Pop, I'd be afraid that he would have a stroke. Mom always tells me to talk to her, but I'm pretty certain that most mothers don't want to hear about their teenage son's erectile dysfunction. Here's how that conversation will go:

Me: Hey mom. I need to talk to you.

Mom (being all excited because she gets to mother and therapize me at the same time): Of course, Dev. What's up?

Me: I can't fuck my girlfriend.

Mom: Oh, honey. I can help you with that.

Me: Okay. What do I do?

Mom: Does everything work? Are you nervous, honey? It's perfectly normal to be nervous.

Me: Yes, Mom. Everything works. I don't think I'm nervous, but maybe I am.

Mom: If you think you're nervous, you probably are. Do you want to start meditating with me in the mornings?

Me: No thanks. I'll figure it out.

Mom: Even though I don't have a penis, I can still understand what you're going through.

Me: No, you can't.

Mom: I am sorry you feel that way. But remember that I am always here for you, and I love you very much. And I am proud of you, whether or not you can complete coitus.

I don't mean to shit on Mom, but she's not a man. She cannot possibly know what it's like to not be able to get a hard-on when you desperately want one! But my dad is not here, and talking to Pops is off the table, and I sure as hell am not talking to my friends. They'll laugh and probably put it on Instagram or some shit. So this is one of the numerous reasons that a kid needs their dad. Here's another one: Father/Son Golf Outings. Here's another one: Watching football. Do you know what it's like to watch an Eagles game with Mom? It's torture! She compliments both teams and then feels bad when someone gets hurt or a player misses a field goal. And it *does not* matter which team. I try to explain to her that Eagles fans do not give a shit about the other teams. But she says that even the Cowboys deserve understanding and kindness. People have no fucking idea what I am living with here!

Mom is always trying to get me to have a relationship with Shawn, but that's not going to happen. He's a nice guy and all, but there's no way that he will replace my dad. I am almost eighteen and not about to share any personal shit with my mom's boyfriend, who is also my best friend's father. I imagine what my dad would think of this turn of

                    Anna Picari

events. I wonder if he'd be happy that Mom found a decent-looking doctor to hang out with. I'd be so pissed if I died and Zory started dating someone else. But since everyone always says that my dad was such an outstanding person, he's probably sitting there on his heaven cloud applauding every time Shawn fucks his wife.

All my life I had goals, even before I knew what a goal was. I remember wanting to learn to ride a bike without my training wheels before I turned five. And I did. I remember deciding to win the fifth-grade spelling bee, and I did. I remember wanting to be at the top of my graduating class, and here I sit. Princeton is my next goal. And if I'm being perfectly honest, marrying Zory would be the ultimate goal.

Kim

Last night, Deven asked if he could eat Thanksgiving at Zory's house. I told him that he could, but they had to come back here to have dessert. Sure, I was disappointed, but I know what it's like to be young and in love. And how important it is to impress your girlfriend or boyfriend's parents. Besides that, dessert is the best part of the day. I ordered an Italian cookie tray from Altomonte's as well as several authentic pastries. My mom was born in Italy and came to the United States as a baby. English was her second language, and she currently spends a lot of time at the famous Philly Italian Market purchasing meats, vegetables, and homemade bread, all while using her language skills. She also knows authentic Italian food, which means that I know authentic Italian food. My maiden name is Smith. Boring, I know, but I never had to spell it for anyone. My dad insists he is an honorary Italian since he has been married to my mom for almost forty-five years, and as a matter of fact, he makes a delectable ricotta pie, which we'll eat with the other desserts. Shawn dropped off a pumpkin pie earlier in the day. I think it was an excuse to make out with me for a few minutes, but I certainly didn't mind, knowing he would be coming to dinner later.

Deven and Zory arrived around six and immediately join us around the table. Kana asks them if they want espresso, and Oliver answers for them by shaking his head forcefully and making a face. But it's too late. Kana doesn't wait for a response and heads over to the larger of my two espresso pots. The television is on mute, and my nearest and dearest are chatting and laughing and eating. I want to cry with happiness. I stand and clink my wineglass with an espresso spoon to draw attention. My glass has not been empty since ten this morning and I wobble slightly.

"I want to thank you all for coming to Thanksgiving dinner. I am grateful for each and every one of you. You are a blessing to me and my family. I love you all," I manage to get out as my voice catches and a wave of tears overcomes me. My mother, Kana, and Julia jump up and hug me, and everyone else either smiles broadly or throws kisses my way. It has been the very best Thanksgiving.

Oliver

My dad makes me go to Deven's house for Thanksgiving dinner, and that loser isn't even here. Of course not, he's at Zory's house. I never get to see that dude unless it's at basketball tryouts. Sometimes I get the impression he's avoiding me. I asked him to go to the movies last weekend and he said he would let me know and then never let me know. There was zero chance I was going to remind him. Fuck him if he can't remember that he was supposed to get back to me.

I don't think I'm going to make the team but will probably be offered a bullshit job like equipment manager. Deven was asked to be team captain, so he is guaranteed a slot. To be honest, he deserves to make the team and to be captain. He's a good guy and a great player. For a high school player. Last year, he kind of figured out that he wouldn't be playing in college, and I think he was relieved. The team list will be posted next Monday when we get back from Thanksgiving break. Either way, I don't care. I don't give a fuck about anything these days. I stopped taking the Zoloft after about four weeks. I did not like how it made me feel. And I was fucking tired of people asking me if I was okay. I guess I looked like I was pissed off all the time. But wasn't that what they were supposed to help me *not* look like? I still talk to Megan every two weeks, and she reminds me at the end of every session about the contract that I signed.

Some days, I want to rip that shit up. Not that it matters. Megan has a copy, and my dad has a copy. I still think about the ways that I can kill myself. The best way that I can think of is parking in the garage and then turning the car on. It would be an epic death. I could have music blasting and then just go to sleep. I would just have to make sure that my dad was not home. I wouldn't want him to get sick. I've decided that he's decent and deserves to live long and be happy.

I call Ms. O "Kim" when we're not in school. It was weird at first, but she made me feel comfortable, so I call her Kim all the time. Sometimes, if I see her in the hallway, I shout, "Hey Kim!" and start laughing. She laughs, too, and just waves me off. I am happy that she is with my dad. They seem like they fit together in a way that he and my mom never did.

My mom looks great today, but I am freaked out that she will relapse. When we have a few minutes alone, I ask her, "Mom, how are you? Really?"

Mom faces me and rubs both of my arms, like she used to when I was little. For a second, I think she isn't going to answer me, but she finally says, "My sweet Oliver. I feel better every day, and having you in my life gives me the strength to stay clean. I love you so much and I hope that you know that."

I feel tears well up and I try to swallow but I can't. Tears are coming, and I feel embarrassed, but Mom just pulls me into a hard hug and I don't ever want to let go of her. I imagine that if I keep hugging her, she won't be able to use again. I whisper into the side of her head in a squeaky voice, "I love you, Mom." She hugs me harder than I thought was possible and we stay that way for a while. And I don't care who's watching.

When we let go, I remind myself that it's Thanksgiving and she isn't drinking and seems normal—or whatever is normal for her. Megan reminds me a lot that worrying about my mom won't make her not use and not worrying about her will make her use. I get that, but it's hard to shake. When I worry about something, it's like I expect it, so then I won't be devastated when it happens. Megan is probably right, though, especially because she has a license and all, but I feel better worrying.

I haven't really seen Z outside of school, and it's great to see her at Thanksgiving. She is a *real* person, you know? And she's really into Deven, that's for sure. I'm not interested in anyone. I still miss Sophia. We only dated for a short time, but I felt really close to her. I felt safe letting her get to know the real me, and then I ruined it. She deserves better.

Oliver

It's the middle of the night and someone is banging on the front door. Dad's actually home, and we both stumble into the hall at the same time. Dad waves for me to stay behind him, and I almost laugh. I am so much bigger than he is, by at least three inches. Dad's fumbling for his phone to check the front door video as he leads our tiny train.

And then he just sighs, and I swear to God, he looks like a balloon actively deflating in front of me. I look over his shoulder at the phone and see Mom. Dad opens the door and Mom practically falls into his arms.

Fuck. She's high.

We bring her to the couch, and she's mumbling something and crying and falling asleep all at the same time. I am so pissed off that I feel like grabbing her and throwing her out. I want to throw shit, punch someone, cry. I must look a little crazy because Dad asks me if I'm okay.

Am I okay? Fuck no! I am not okay. This is such bullshit.

The motherfucking inevitable has happened.

As soon as I started to relax about Mom dying from an overdose, she fucking starts this shit again. I am so goddamned mad that my head might explode.

Dad tries to put his arm around me, but I slap it away and head to my room, slamming the door behind me. I plop down on my bed and cover my face with a pillow. I get up and throw a framed picture of me and Mom from my nightstand across the room. The force of my throw and the weirdly satisfying crash of the picture frame prompts me to keep throwing shit. I throw anything I can get my hands on—shoes, some vintage vinyl, an old soccer ball.

The LEGO Millennium Falcon is sitting on a special shelf. I'm walking to it as Dad opens my door. He says, "No, Oliver. That took you weeks." I can't remember what I say back to him, but I put my arm on the shelf next to it, and with all my might, I swipe it off the shelf and into the wall, and it crumbles into a pile of LEGO shit. Before I realize what's happening, I bend down to pick it up and start bawling. I'm screaming while punching at the pile of LEGOs.

Dad gets on the floor and grabs my hands because they're bleeding now. Snot is dripping out of my nose, but I don't give a shit. I use my arm to wipe it like a kindergarten kid does. Dad goes to hug me but I jump up.

"I am going back to bed," I say.

"Okay. I love you, Ol."

"Me too," I say.

Dad leaves, and I fall back onto my bed, close my eyes, and start sobbing again.

My life sucks. Some days, it's hard to even get up and ready for school. I just want to stay in my bed with the covers pulled over my head. And cry. I cry more than a guy my age should. I don't give a shit about anything. My grades. Basketball. College. I don't even care about Sophia anymore. I feel numb about everything. I feel nothing and unbelievable pain at the same time on most days. I can't even explain the pain. It's as if all the horrible things happening in the universe are in my brain at the same time, and my brain doesn't know what to do, so it shoots it all through my body so that my body can feel all these horrible things. When Megan asks me what the pain feels like, I just say that I can't explain it because I don't want her to think I'm losing my mind. At the end of every session, she tells me she is proud of me, and I just mumble something back. I know she's trying so hard to fix me, but I don't think she can.

                                        Anna Picari

Kim

As I'm getting ready for work on this slow-moving morning of the Monday after the Thanksgiving holiday, my cell phone rings. I smile as I see his picture pop onto my phone screen while the ringtone of "Bad Case of Loving You" by Robert Palmer plays.

"Doctor, doctor. Give me the news," I sometimes joke when I answer his calls, but today I just say, "Good morning, Shawn."

"Hey, Kim. I can't stay on long, but I want you to know that Aubrey relapsed last night, and I am going to try to get her back in treatment this morning. Oliver is not taking this well."

"I am so sorry," I say and then add, "I will have eyes on Oliver. Please let me know if there's anything I can do."

"I will. Thanks, babe. I love you," Shawn said.

"I love you, too," and I hit the end button on my phone. And for a split second, I am annoyed that Shawn still has to deal with this. I am proud of him and irritated at the same time. Aubrey has a sister who lives in Montgomery County, for crying out loud. But then I reprimanded myself for being bothered. Shawn and Aubrey share a history and have managed to remain good friends through all the drama. I finish getting dressed and head downstairs. Deven and Julia are toasting bagels.

"Oh, good. Mom. Do you want to go halfsies with me? These bagels are huge!" Jules asks.

"It's not a chocolate chip bagel, is it?" I ask, making a face. Julia shares that it's a cinnamon raisin bagel as I head to the coffee pot. Deven is looking down at his phone.

"Yo, Dev. No phones when we're eating."

"I know, Mom. But Oliver posted something weird on IG."

Deven holds his phone so that I can see Oliver's post. It's only four words: TAKE ME TO HELL in red bold letters on a black background with something resembling flames surrounding it.

"And he's not answering my texts," Deven adds, the worry evident in his face.

I tell him that I will call him to my office as soon as school starts, and this seems to put Deven at ease. I am, however, more than a little uneasy.

Julia and I arrive at school. I've been dropping her off at the middle school drop-off point so she no longer is seen walking into school with her mother or her older brother. Her sessions with Kristy seem to be helping our relationship. She's extremely open with me. Sometimes, perhaps too open. For example, last week she walked down the stairs in an odd way. I asked her why she was walking like that, and she responded that she had "borrowed" one of my tampons. This led to a discussion about whether a person should feel the tampon once it's in. I emphatically replied, "No!" She asked me if I could show her how to use one, and I laughed and said, "No. But I will coach you through it."

We went to my bathroom, and I settled myself on the floor, looking away from the toilet, leaning on the side of the tub. After several attempts, Julia got it. We were so happy, we high-fived and hugged. Talk about an authentic mother-daughter bonding experience. I was too embarrassed to ask my mom, so I didn't use tampons until I was in high school. A friend told me how to do it one day after PE, but it was awkward in the girls' bathroom stall right next to the girls' locker room. I swear that everyone could hear me whine, "I can't find the hole. Which hole? Where is the hole?"

I park my car in my spot. I have a reserved parking spot near the front of the elementary school: Ms. Kim Orsetti, LCSW. I have a clin-

 Anna Picari

ical license that I only used for two years after licensure. I worked in a small office in Center City, Philadelphia, and saw clients. I really liked my clients but had a hard time charging them for the sessions. Many of those who came in did not have the funds to pay the seventy-five-dollar per session fee, and I ended up doing a lot of reduced-fee or pro-bono counseling. Needless to say, it was not a lucrative business. When I was near the end of my pregnancy with Deven, I decided to close the office. I wanted to stay at home for at least a year with my baby, but I kept my license current. I applied to Freedom when Deven was two, and I never looked back. Working in a school is perfect for a parent, and I love the culture and the climate of my school.

Within a quarter of an hour, I'm walking into the building when I hear, "Good morning, Kim." It's Marla, our business manager extraordinaire.

"Hey there, Mar! How is that gorgeous granddaughter of yours?"

"Absolutely perfect," Marla answers, and we fall into step as we go into the building together. Marla shares with me that there was a board of trustee meeting later that morning. Charter schools run more like a business than a traditional school. Freedom Charter feels nothing like a business. The teachers, administrators, and students are free to be themselves but with the expectation of total effort at all times. There is an air of respect and kindness because of it.

We say our goodbyes as Marla heads to her office, which is located adjacent to Mandy's office, and I head to my office. There are four fifth-grade girls waiting for me, and I usher them into my office with a smile as I take off my pink parka. About twenty-five minutes later, I turn on my laptop to send a notification for Oliver to come to my office before lunch, but he was marked "Absent, Unexcused." I look at Oliver's schedule and call his first-period classroom. The teacher informs me that he hasn't yet arrived at class. I then use my office phone to call Shawn, but he doesn't pick up. Is he still working on getting a placement for Aubrey? Did he have surgeries scheduled? I quickly call his office and am told he wouldn't be in the office until the afternoon. I hang up my office phone, pick it up again, and dial Oliver's cell, and it goes straight to voicemail. I then try calling Oliver from my cell. No answer. I grab my handbag and parka, leaving my backpack, and head to the front door. I stick my head in the office and tell them that I'm doing a well-check on a student and leave before someone asks me for the name of the student.

Pulling up to the McDaniels' house, I feel unnerved. I look for Oliver's car, which is Aubrey's old car. He parks it directly in front of the house, if there's a spot to be had. I look up and down the street in case he had to park somewhere else, but the car is not there. I leave my purse in the car, bringing only my keys and phone. I knock on the door. I ring the doorbell. I have a key to Shawn's house, but I want to show some respect in case Oliver is in the shower or something. I knock again. Still no answer. I use my key and step inside and call: "Oliver. Oliver. Are you here?"

Oliver

I hear Kim. What the hell? Why the fuck is she here? Even though I'm in the garage, I try to calm my breathing, thinking she can hear me. Sometimes, I'm just dumb like that. The garage is in the back of the house. Our house was once what's known as a "tear-down." That means that the original house was gutted and voila. Our house was built from the ashes. The house is one of two houses in our neighborhood with a garage. I am sitting in my car in the garage. Dad parks his Tesla here one hundred percent of the time, but he's gone, taking Mom to another rehab. This is a space worthy of Dad's nearly 100G, Tesla Model S. The garage is spotless and painted a light blue color, like the color of the sky. I think of the garage as the "car room," not a garage. Kim is calling louder now. I hear her walking through the house, and I am glad that I did not start the car yet. I wouldn't want to hurt her or anyone, for that matter. I look down at the four envelopes that sit on the passenger seat. *Dad. Mom. Megan. Deven.* And I wonder whether I should have written a letter to Kim, too.

Kim

I knock gently on Oliver's bedroom door and then open it when no one answers. I peer inside and take a look around. The room is oddly tidy and clean. Strange. Teenage boys are not known for being neat. But he's not here. I look in Shawn's room and the kitchen. No Oliver. I sit at the kitchen table and call the office to see if Oliver arrived. He has not. Then I called Shawn. He answers.

"Shawn, is Oliver with you?" I ask, trying to keep panic out of my voice.

"No. Why? Isn't he at school?" Shawn's voice rises as he asks the question. I explained that Oliver hadn't come to school and that I was at their house, seeing if he was there. Shawn asked if Oliver's car was on the street, and I told him that it wasn't. "I am almost out of here. I'll call you when I'm on my way." And he hangs up.

I make sure the door is locked when I leave. I'm going to check the park and the shopping center where the kids like to hang out before heading back to school.

Oliver

I think that I hear Kim leave, so I check my Ring app and see her walking away from the door. I remember reading somewhere that I should open a window in the house, so I head back into the house and open the big kitchen window. Then I head back to the garage. I take a breath and get in. I sit in Mom's old car, and for an instant, I wonder if I can get better, feel better. But I have tried everything that Megan suggested. The only exception is that I bailed on the medication. At first my dad would watch me take it, but after about two weeks, he trusted me. I put my head in my hands and then fold forward onto the steering wheel, knowing that I let him down. And everyone else, too. But think about being free from this pain, from this gripping emptiness soon. And that thought propels me. I turn the key.

Oliver

Dear Dad,

I am so sorry. There was no other way out for me. I cannot keep living like this. Please know that there is nothing you could have done. I would have found another way to get rid of this pain. You have been a great dad. I love you so much, and I am so happy that you have Kim. She is really great, and I hope that you have a great life together. I will remember all the fun times we had from wherever I am, probably sitting on the edge of Saturn's ring, watching you. I promise to only watch the PG stuff.

You are a great dad. Thank you for giving me a good life.

Love Always,

Oliver

Dear Mom,

Please do not blame yourself. I just can't do this anymore. My mind is full and empty at the same, and my heart feels shattered. You were the best mom, and I am so grateful for everything. And even though I said that you were embarrassing, you weren't. I secretly loved all the notes that you left in my lunchbox.

You always say that I will always be your baby. But you will always be my mommy. Always, Mom! I love you to the moon and back and more than this much and to infinity and beyond.

Love Always,

Oliver

PS. Try to stay clean. You deserve to be happy.

Dear Megan,

You are cooler than I ever thought a therapist could be. I am sorry that I broke our contract, but you, above all, know the pain that is with me all day. Every single day. This is not your fault. I know that there are a lot of people that you help, so please keep doing that. They need you. The world needs people like you. You are amazing and helpful at your job, and don't let this make you think any different.

From,

Oliver

Dear Deven,

You are my brother. I would not have survived as long as I did if I never met you. Please do NOT beat yourself up over this. I know you. You feel responsible for everything. But you are not responsible for this. I am. I need to take care of myself, and this is the only way out.

Go to Princeton—Marry Zory (or some other hottie that you meet at college). Have a ton of babies. Make a jillion dollars. Give to charity AND vacation in Thailand. You deserve a big life because you have a big heart. Make your life mean something because you mean something.

I love you, man.

Oliver

Kim

As I head back to the office, I think about where Oliver could be. I cannot think of a single place other than home or school or the park. I make the decision to talk to Deven as soon as I get to school.

Several minutes later, I'm back in my parking spot. I quickly grab my purse and head inside. I haphazardly wave to the office staff as I book it to my office. I quickly send Deven an appointment notice for ASAP. ASAP appointments are for emergencies. As I'm pacing in my office, my cell phone rings. It's Shawn, and I exhale and let my shoulders fall from my ears the smallest bit. I slide the bar to answer with a shaking hand.

"Kim, any sight of him?"

"No, Shawn. I'm going to talk to Deven in a minute. Where are you?" I ask, trying not to sound frantic. Shawn explains that he just dropped Aubrey at a rehab an hour away, in Glasgow, Delaware. He should be home in less than an hour. I tell him I would like to text Megan to see if she's heard from him and ask Shawn for consent. He quickly agrees and I ask, "They had a contract, didn't they?"

Shawn sighs and says, "Yes, but that doesn't mean anything. It was just to take liability away from the therapist. I don't think Oliver would ever hurt himself."

I have to bite my tongue to keep from shouting at him. He's a medical professional. How could he be so cavalier about suicidal ideation?

Shawn adds, "He's probably at the park or by the river. I'll check there when I get in town. I just wish that he'd answer his goddamn phone."

Yeah, me too, I think as I say goodbye to Shawn and straight away text Megan.

Have you heard from O. McD?

Less than a minute later, my phone rings. As soon as I answer, Megan asks, "What's going on?" I am distractedly pacing my office as I fill her in. The thing about therapists is that you can tell them anything you want, but they cannot tell you anything without a signed release of information. Megan listens, thanks me, and asks me to notify her if anything changes. After we hang up, I wonder if Megan will notify the authorities, which wouldn't be the worst idea.

I do my best thinking while walking, and I almost walk right into Deven as he enters my office.

"What's up, Mom?"

I don't have time to mince words: "We can't find Oliver." I give a quick rundown of what has been happening and finally say, "Please tell me you've heard from him."

Deven just shakes his head and sits on my couch. I move right next to him and ask if there's somewhere he could have gone. Deven lowers his head as he starts texting someone.

He notices me looking over his shoulder. "I'm asking Z or Sophia if they heard from him." The negative responses come quickly, and I tell him to tell them not to worry because he probably just has his phone turned off. Deven does as I ask and then leans back on the couch, with his head resting on the top. "Do you think he's okay?"

I answer honestly. "I hope so, but I have no idea."

I settle down next to my handsome boy. Deven will bear a big burden if something happens to his friend. He asks if he can stay with me for a while, and I add him to the "excused" list. I tell Deven he's welcome to stay in my office while I notify Dr. Perry and make my way to her office.

Mandy waves me in when she sees me in the door, and I immediately tell her what's going on with Oliver. She sits there quietly and listens to every word. Then she asks, "What do you think?" and I start to cry because I am imagining the worst, that he threw himself off a bridge or off an overpass or somehow commandeered a firearm. I know what clinical depression looks like, and Oliver could be the poster child. Mandy then asks me what she could do to help, and I tell her I would let her know if I needed anything. She rubs my shoulders as I leave, and I feel worse, not better. Usually when I share something about a student with Mandy, I feel lighter somehow. But not this time. Oliver is much more than a student to me. This time, telling Mandy made it real.

Deven

A million thoughts are racing through my head. Where the fuck is Oliver? He wouldn't do something stupid, would he? Nah, he's not that selfish. But Mom has her worried face on, and that makes me worry. I've been texting Zory, and she keeps saying that he's probably drunk somewhere. That does not make me feel any better.

I think about when Oliver and I were little kids. We went back and forth between our houses, making messes and eating all kinds of junk food. Well, at least at Oliver's house we ate junk food. Aubrey would serve chips and soda, while my mom would always have strawberries or sliced apples. You would have thought she'd get the hint since we *never* ate any of the fruit that she put out for us. I imagine my dad would have served us pretzels and dip or chips and salsa, if he was around. I know that he never met Oliver, and he has changed a lot recently. He's the funniest human being in the world. You know how a drink will come out of your nose if you start laughing really hard while you're drinking? Oliver can do that on demand! I have no idea how, but he can take a slug of any drink and have it exit through his nose. He brags that he knows how to do that because his dad is an ENT. I think he's full of shit, but that's what makes Oliver Oliver. Lately, he's been depressed. At least that's what Mom says, and she knows what she's talking about when it comes to this shit, at least.

Oliver texted me yesterday after I got done with basketball practice. He wasn't there because I think he can see the writing on the wall. I really hope he doesn't do something bad. It's as if he can't do anything to keep his mind off the sadness. I'm worried about him. Mom thinks he should be on suicide watch or something, but she assumes that about anyone who's really depressed. I don't think he'll kill himself. He wouldn't do that to his parents or to me, but he has *really* got to lighten up. Last week, he tried to give me a football with Donovan McNabb's autograph on it. It was weird, and when I asked him why he wanted to give the football away, he said, "I don't know. I just don't need it anymore." That was a dumb thing to say. Who really ever *needs* an autographed football?

My mind transitions back to places that Oliver could be just as Mom comes back into her office.

Kim

Deven looks more nervous than I have ever seen him. When he sees me, his face is hopeful for a second. I sit next to him and glance at his phone. He just shakes his head. We sit in what feels like interminable silence, but in reality, it's only about twenty seconds. Deven superfluously peeks at his phone again and says, "Where the hell is he?"

"I don't know, babe."

"And everywhere has been checked?" he asks for confirmation.

"I checked the park and his house."

Deven asks if I saw his car, and I said that it wasn't on the street.

"Did you look in the garage?" he asks offhandedly.

I mentally berate myself for not thinking that Oliver could have moved his car into the garage.

I jump up faster than I knew I could move, grab my purse, and yell for Deven to follow. I call Shawn and ask him if he can access the garage remotely. I breathe a sigh of relief as he confirms that he has an app and he'll open the garage door for us right away. He tells me that he's going to call for emergency response, just in case.

Oliver

I feel at peace. Like I am floating on a cloud. Then, somewhere in the darkest parts of my brain, I hear the garage door open.

Kim

I have never broken more traffic laws than I did today. I don't give a shit. We get to Shawn's house in less than fifteen minutes and pull into the alleyway behind the row of houses. Deven is out of the car before I even put the car in park. I catch up with him as he bangs on the driver's side window, trying to get Oliver to wake up. Through terrified tears, Deven screams, "Wake up! Oliver, wake the fuck up!"

I glance around the garage to find something to smash the window with. "Jesus Christ!" I yell as I look around the space. There's nothing in here other than the car. I hurriedly run into the adjacent laundry room. Nothing. I run into the kitchen and grab the fire extinguisher from under the sink.

I swiftly return to the garage and begin to use the extinguisher to smash the back driver's side window. Deven yanks it out of my hand and, with the force, strength, and sheer will of an eighteen-year-old, hoists it over his right shoulder and smashes it into the window. In what appears to be ice shattering on a frozen pond, the window momentarily looks elegant and ethereal.

Without a second to lose, Deven, filled with adrenaline, climbs on top of the car and hangs his legs over the shattered window. With only three hard backward kicks, he busts the window open, just as the sound of sirens fills the space.

Deven

It's like I'm watching someone else. A surreal out-of-body experience. I'm moving on instinct. This is what survival mode looks like. If Oliver dies, I know that I will die, too.

When the window glass finally flies free, I slide off the top of the car, find the inside side panel, and open the door. I maneuver myself into the front and unlock the driver's side door. Mom's there, ready to go.

I push myself out of the passenger door, willing my brain to unsee the envelope with DEVEN written on it, and meet Mom at the driver's door. We twist Oliver's limp body so that we can each have an arm, and lower him to the garage floor.

I drop down and pick Oliver up like he's a baby or something. I rock and shake him forcefully, trying to wake him up, as something that sounds like a screeching wail comes out of me. I think I hear him grumble as the EMTs rush in.

Kim

I follow the ambulance to Temple University Hospital with Shawn on Bluetooth as I keep pace with the rescue vehicle. Deven is speed-texting with Zory and Sophia, I guess. I shot Mandy a text update right before I called Shawn, who must have been out of his mind with fear and worry. He tells me that he's only fifteen minutes away and will meet us at the Emergency Department.

Oliver

I feel lightheaded, and I know my eyes are closed. Something is tickling my nose, and my mouth is dry and pasty. I can hear people talking, but I can't make out exactly who is with me or what they're saying. Where am I? I feel like I can open my eyes, but I don't want to. Think. The last thing I remember is sitting in my car, feeling peaceful.

Oh, shit. My mind is suddenly more alert, but I stay perfectly still. I hear my dad and . . . my mom?

Mom?

Shouldn't she be in Delaware? I can't be sure because everyone is whispering.

Wait. I think I remember now.

I am such a fucking fuck-up! I cannot believe that I messed up!

I feel like throwing up, but I swallow it down. I don't want anyone to know that I'm awake.

I wish I was dead. That was the plan.

The vomit is now a force to pay attention to. I turn my head to the side and vomit. And then vomit again. I keep my eyes closed, but somehow I know people are staring at me. I can feel it. But I just drift away.

And the silence . . . where is all the talking? The silence is strange. I begin to wonder if I did die. But then I hear movement, but I purposely choose to stay with my head turned in case of someone seeing me. But before long, my mom rushes to my side, slipping on the vomit. She didn't seem to notice as we make eye contact, and she grabs my face in her hands and kisses me.

"Oh, my sweet boy," Mom says as I close my eyes again. Maybe if I keep my eyes closed, everyone will leave, and I'll be back in the garage.

I have to think, but my brain is too foggy to think at all. But to be honest, I like the way it feels. I think I go out again, but when I wake, I can smell Mom's soap, which is competing with another weird smell that has been lingering in my nose since I woke up. I gradually open my eyes and see Dad. And he looks directly at me. He looks old—I mean, like he got older since I saw him this morning—and it freaks me out. I have never seen him look like that before.

Kim

Oliver is awake, and I want to cry tears of joy and relief. The whole day was surreal. I cannot stop replaying the whole scene in my mind. The broken windshield, the EMTs, the sirens on the ambulance. The sound of relief and worry as I told Shawn that we had gotten to Oliver and that he was still alive. But what I didn't tell Shawn was that Oliver was only semiconscious at first and then went out. Deven's face wore a look of total fear. He understandably freaked out, and I don't think he even realized tears were running down his face.

Before getting into the car to follow the ambulance, I grabbed the four envelopes that were on the passenger seat and shoved them in my purse. Deven saw me do this but didn't say a word. I'll give them back to Oliver at some point. I'll tell Shawn about them, too. Those envelopes will make it real, but if anyone needs a punch-in-the-gut reality check, it's Shawn.

Four hours later, Oliver finally turns his head so that it's facing the ceiling, but his eyes open and then close. I ask Shawn and Aubrey if they want a few minutes alone with their son. Shawn nods, and I grab my purse and go to find Deven.

Deven is sitting in the family waiting room. Somehow, Zory and Sophia are sitting next to him, one on each side. He jumps up when he sees me. "Is Oliver okay?"

I take a breath and say that I think so, but the doctors would be running tests.

"What kind of tests?" Deven asks anxiously.

I explain that we have no idea how long Oliver was breathing in carbon monoxide and that he could have some lasting residual effects. Deven looks like he's going to cry again, and I quickly try to deflect.

"He is awake, and it's a good sign that he recognized his parents."

This seems to assuage Deven's fears, and he just nods and asks when he can see him. I share that I didn't think Oliver would be up to visitors today and that maybe Zory and Sophia should just head home. The girls take the hint and get up. Deven stands and hugs both and tells them that he'll talk to them later.

After the girls get on the elevator to leave, Deven wraps his arms around me and begins to weep. I keep rubbing his back and holding my boy, this young man, as if he's a toddler. I don't want to let him go. Ever. If he stays in my arms forever, nothing bad will ever happen to him.

Eventually, I say, "Let's head home." Deven is too emotionally wrecked to argue. I keep my arm around his waist as we walk to the car.

Deven

I hesitate as I go to open the passenger door of Mom's car. I remember the envelopes on the passenger seat of Oliver's car. And I think about how one of them has my name on it. It's weird that my brain held on to this until now. I open the door and get in.

"Mom, did you see the envelopes in the car?"

Mom doesn't even play dumb. "Yes. I saw them."

"Do you think they're suicide notes or something?"

Mom just nods and tells me she has them. I ask her if I can have the one for me.

"Deven, no. Your very good friend is experiencing such intense pain. I don't think he would have written any of them if he had been stable. And besides, they're not mine. I'm going to give them back to him when he's ready for them."

"What if he's never ready for them?" I ask. And Mom just reaches over and grabs my hand, never answering my question.

When we get home, Julia is there with Gram and Pops. Gram immediately hugs me and whispers in my ear that she's very proud of me. And I want to cry again but I hold it in. I just break away and announce that I'm heading to my room. I plop down on my bed and cover my eyes with my arm. I replay what happened this morning. Again and again. What the hell was Oliver doing? I am one hundred percent sure it wasn't an accident.

Those envelopes told me that. What made him want to kill himself? He seemed like he was less depressed, like he was finally over Sophia and wanted to move on. I don't get it. Was he faking it? I don't know what to believe. I think about Shawn's face when he finally made it to the hospital. That man was shattered. That's the only way I can describe it. He looked like Shawn but looked like a ghost of Shawn at the same time. He hugged and thanked me. I didn't know what to say back, so I just stood there, my arms hanging by my side. Shawn's a decent enough guy, so I let him hold me awkwardly, feeling his pain.

I text Z, saying thanks for coming to hang with me at the hospital. She just sends a heart emoji. I send one back and drop my phone on my bed. I'm thirsty so I head downstairs. I overhear my mom telling my grandparents that she's worried that Oliver could have brain damage.

"Even though I know all the science of suicide, I can't help but feel inadequate and ineffectual."

Gram just puts her hand on top of Mom's hand and squeezes it just as I hit the bottom step. All three of them look up at me, like they don't know who I am, but I just go to the fridge and grab a Pepsi.

Mom says, "Pizza should be here in about ten."

I say okay and head back upstairs to my room, but not without swiping those envelopes from mom's purse first. As soon as I get to my room, I fall back on my bed as I open the envelope with my name on it.

Dear Deven,

You are my brother. I would not have survived as long as I did if I never met you.

I can't get past that first sentence. My eyes are filled with tears, and I can't see the next words. I don't know if I want to see them. I drop the paper on the floor, and I just lie there with huge fucking tears dripping down my face. I'm rubbing my hands up and down my face.

"What the fuck, Oliver?" I ask out loud.

I grab my laptop and google "signs of suicide." I click on the first thing on my search. It's the Suicide Prevention Resource Center, and as soon as I click on it, the number 988 catches my eye. It's the number for the Suicide Prevention hotline or something, and I know that I will never forget this number until the day I die. The lists of warning signs are right there, and I feel sick as I read them. How did everyone miss this? Oliver checked every, single, fucking box. I read about protective factors versus risk factors and commit them all to memory. For some weird reason, I feel energized. If I'm his brother, then he's going to feel the full force of my protective factor.

I pick up his letter and open a blank doc on my laptop. I'm writing one back to him.

Dear Oliver Xavier McDaniel,

You are my brother as well. You make my life better in a lot of ways. I don't have to pretend that I have my shit together all the time when it's just the two of us hanging out. And I plan to hang out with you at the retirement home one day, far in the future. The old ladies will be all over our wrinkly, big dicks.

I love you, but I am pissed off at you. You have so much to offer this world, but you gotta stick around to make that happen. Happy Valley needs you! And I need to visit you there and experience what all the hype is about.

Promise me that you will tell me with actual words if you ever feel like ending things again. I will be right there. I am forever here for you, brother.

I love you.

Deven Matthew Orsetti

I fold the letter and write OLIVER on the outside of the paper. I run downstairs and put the remaining three envelopes back in Mom's bag. I will explain that I borrowed my letter so that I could write a retort. And then I smile—this is exactly something that Mom would tell me to do. I remember one time when I was really upset about a classmate calling me "Spaghetti, Orsetti" and Mom told me to write him a note saying I didn't like to be called that. It's at times like these that I really appreciate my mom.

                                            Anna Picari

Oliver

I become more alert as the day drags on. And on. And on. And on. This doctor. That doctor. This doctor prescribes this medication. This nurse administers that medication. I like that nurse. Her name is Carson, and I think that's a cool name. So, I instantly decide that she is a cool nurse. And she is very cute.

The psychiatrist (who told me that I could call him Dr. Joe) asks to speak to me alone. He holds out a clipboard with a paper on it for me to sign so that he has permission to talk to Megan. I sign it. My dad spoke to Megan already. He tells me he called her while he was driving home from Delaware and that she was very relieved when he called back later and told her that I should be okay.

Dr. Joe explains that I will be in the hospital for at least two more days, and then there will be a team meeting about me. The team is composed of Dr. Joe, Nurse Carson, the hospital social worker Dr. Messelberg, my parents, and Megan. Dr. Joe asks if I wanted to include anyone else. *Hell no.* I don't even want to include the people that have to be included! I don't want anyone else stuck in this misery. But I will play the game if it means that I can get out of here faster.

I feel like I'm a prisoner, and I feel like I have been hit with a dose of THC and that I could fall asleep at any time.

Dr. Joe finally leaves to talk to my parents, who are out in the hallway, pacing, I bet. I close my eyes, enjoying the high, plans forming in my mind.

Julia

Girls Rule #6

Mr. Jabs A Lot. Today, I didn't have a funny name to call you, so I thought this one was funny. But I have a question for you . . . why does your name have a random letter *f*? It would sound better without it—just one person's opinion. And it makes your name much harder to say. I told Kristy that I still use your name when I journal, but I am running out of silly ways to write it. She suggested the one I used today. LOL. I think I like this one best. It's saying that girls talk a lot. Mom always says we should never assign a gender to intelligence, strength, or caring, but I don't think jabbering is a bad thing. Lately, I have been jabbering at everyone. I used to be so shy, but not anymore. I like this about myself.

Something weird is going on with Oliver. Do you know Oliver Mc-Daniel? He goes to Freedom. He's my brother's best friend, and he is in the hospital. I don't know why because everyone stops talking when I walk in the room, but I think that it's something bad. Both my mom and Deven looked like they were crying when they came home from the hospital yesterday. But they seemed better this morning when we were getting ready for school.

Once I got in the car, I asked Mom for details, but she just said that Oliver was in an accident, but he would be alright. I asked if he was going to be at school today, and she told me no. Once we got to the car line, she reached over and hugged me really hard and said that I was a blessing every day and that she loved me so much. I told her that I loved her too, trying to get out of the hug since everyone in the middle school was looking at us.

Kim

It's been weeks since Oliver's attempt and things at home and school have been relatively quiet. I am in my office, thinking about how well Oliver seems to be doing, and the phone rings. I look at the ID. It's Mandy. I answer, "Hey there, Mandy. Is this business or pleasure?"

She lets out a chuckle and says, "Pleasure. Definitely." She proceeds to confirm Christmas dinner plans and what she can bring. "Should I make sure I have enough food for about five hundred people?"

"Well," I say. "I didn't invite *that* many people, but I am expecting the entire Eagles' defensive team." I'm smiling as I hang up.

December came in with a bang, that's for sure, but I'm working hard on not letting that get in the way of having a peaceful Christmastime, for all of us. I've been shopping for gifts, happily including Shawn and Oliver on my lists. I will ask for Deven's help with Oliver, but I have zero ideas for Shawn. We have grown even closer since Oliver's episode.

Shawn had asked me to meet him at his house two days after Oliver was hospitalized. He was going to pick up some clothes for Oliver. When he opened the door, I pulled him into my arms and let him cry. Eventually, I led him to the couch and Shawn immediately hugged me. He cried harder, and the next thing we knew, we were pulling and tugging at one another's clothes until we were both completely naked. Our mouths needed to taste every inch of one another. My nipples were raw, and I'm pretty sure I gave Shawn a hickey on his shoulder, but we didn't care. As if by some magnetic force, I found myself straddling Shawn and fucking him like it was the last time. I thought about what he almost lost, of what I had lost, of how I found love again. He met every penetration with hard thrusts, and I cried out just as he let out a final moan. This was the kind of sex people have after a tragedy—raw and needy and desperate. It's the kind of sex that makes us feel something, although it seems counterintuitive. This is the reason 9/11 babies were conceived; we needed to feel connected amid one of the greatest tragedies our country has experienced. Our collective trauma required a release.

We lay together for a long time and talked about the events in the car and what the plan for Oliver was moving forward. Shawn told me that Oliver would be in the hospital for another day or two and that he would be released to him. He would have to go to therapy with Megan three times a week for two weeks and then twice a week for at least four weeks.

It's been two weeks now, and Shawn still refuses to call it an "attempt," but I do from time to time. That's what it was, and Shawn now has the concreteness of knowing about the notes. Deciding to give the envelopes to Shawn instead of Oliver was a no-brainer. I needed to make sure Shawn fully understood the significance of Oliver's actions. We all need to be vigilant because a person with a prior suicide attempt is more likely to complete suicide the next time.

Shawn gave Megan the envelope with her name, and I know that, being the caring and thoughtful therapist she is, she will review the note with Oliver in a future session. I hope she's conferring with another therapist who specializes in teens with suicidal ideation. My controlling nature is prompting me to call her and make sure, but I've held myself back so far. She's very good at her job. I know. But this is beautiful Oliver. Making the decision to trust that Megan knows what she is doing, I let go the mental list of therapeutic interventions that would be useful. Oliver knows to check-in with me every morning when he arrives and each day before lunch. He seems better. I know that he's on a cocktail of medications, and they seem to be working. Shawn informs me that he watches Oliver take both his morning medication and his evening medication.

I am hosting Christmas Eve this year with my mom as my usual cohost. We will be making the Feast of the Seven Fish, our yearly tradition. Every year, we make shrimp, lobster, crab, mussels, clams, baccalà, and scallops. This is purely an Italian American thing. When my mom had relatives visit from Italy one Christmas, they looked at us like we were crazy when we told them that there would be seven different fish dishes. They laughed at us and told us that, in Italy, there is only one or two fish dishes on Christmas Eve.

People ask, "Why seven fish?" and since I now know that the tradition was only to eat some type of fish to celebrate the birth of Christ, I share an American story that I once heard. This tale is that the fish represents the seven churches people in Italy used to visit on Christmas Eve. I know it's a bold-faced lie, but it sounds more festive.

The usual suspects will be at my house on the twenty-fourth, plus a few special guests. Mandy and her wife usually pop by for some mussels and wine, and I always invite my aunts, uncles, and cousins. It's buffet style, so no one must hurry or feel like they cannot leave early.

I bring my mind back to the present and the colossal amount of work on my desk. I take a deep breath and get to work, visions of sugar plums dancing in my head.

Deven

As soon as I get home from basketball practice, I fly up to my room to check my Princeton decision. The website states that early decision applicants will know of their acceptance/rejection by mid-December. I know that it's early, but I open my application portal, and it's not there today. Damn it. I check social media just to double check, and no one has gotten their decisions. I feel like Schrodinger's fucking cat. Am I admitted? Am I rejected? I can be either one at this point. I guess I'll try again tomorrow.

I text Zory.

hey

did you get a decision?

no, but it's fine. always tomorrow

want to hang out tomorrow night?
at my house. parents out

okay i should be there by 6:30

I lean back on my desk chair and think about being fully and completely alone with Zory. My boner starts the second I imagine kissing her. We've been hooking up since that unfortunate incident with my uncooperative dick. It's always in my car, though, so we haven't tried to actually do IT again. My downstairs friend is cooperating now, that's for sure, and I debate whether I should jerk off or stay completely away from that region until tomorrow night. But my dick is straining against my underwear, so I stand, make sure the door is closed, and think about Zory and what's between her legs as I do my thing.

Julia

Girls Rule #7

Mr. J. Whazzzzzuppppp? I am feeling fun today. I have to get something for Mom. I hope Deven can take me somewhere to Christmas shop on Sunday. I think he will. I don't think he got anything for his gf yet, so he has to go. I am only buying a few gifts. I only have the $150 that my mom gave me for gifts. I am buying a gift for Mom, Deven, OP, Allie, Gram, and Pop. I am excited to have everyone come on Christmas Eve. There are a lot of fish. I only like the shrimp and the lobster. But there is always yummy holiday punch and a lot of snacks. I am going to invite Allie, but she may be with her dad for Christmas. She is now my bff. She has really changed and is a much better friend.

Shawn will probably come too. Mom likes him a lot. I can tell. I asked her if she was going to marry him and she just said that she doesn't know. She never gives me a straight answer on anything interesting. And the other thing about Shawn is that I think that he is sad because something is wrong with Oliver. Once, I overheard Mom and Deven talking and I think he was in the hospital because he wanted to hurt himself. He's home now so he's probs fine.

Deven

I take an enormous breath, shake out my arms like I do after a work-out, and knock on Zory's door. She answers in bare feet, wearing a pair of shorts and her hot-pink Freedom hoodie. She looks amazing. I follow her into the kitchen, and she asks if I want something to drink.

"I'll have a Coke if you have any," I reply. I learned early that Zory comes from a Coca-Cola family. She has the soda in the fancy glass bottles. Once the top is flicked off with the bottle opener, Z hands it to me and refills a water glass that is sitting next to the fridge. We head to her massive living room and turn on the television to an episode of *The Office.* Zory sits right next to me, and I struggle to contain myself because her shorts creep up, and I can see both of her long, light brown legs curled under her. I move my right hand so that it rests on her right leg. God, her skin is like silk. I begin to make small circles with my fingertips. She shifts a little so her legs are not stacked on top of one another anymore, and I take this as a signal that she wants me to move to the inside of her thighs.

All of a sudden, I feel panicked. I have a sudden urge to run out the front door so I won't even have a chance for my dick to fail me.

Get a fucking grip, man! I tell myself as I move my hand to touch the inside of her thighs.

Zory moves her hips away from my side so I now have full access to both thighs. Jim and Pam are chatting on the television while I move my fingertips up and down her thighs. Zory lets out a small moan, and I feel my downstairs friend waking up—big time. I kiss her, and she kisses me back in a way that lets me know she's all in. I manage to keep my hand moving up and down her soft legs, and she kisses me and I am so ready now that I feel like I'm going to explode. In one move, I have her on her back and pull her hoodie over her head and I have to restrain myself from actually devouring her.

I am so excited by her and by the fact that I don't have to join the priesthood or some shit. Nature did not fail me.

When we finish, Zory rolls off me and onto the floor beside where I'm lying, still trying to catch my breath. She kisses me gently and whispers, "I love you."

I pull her into a hug. "I love you, too," I say quietly into her hair, a freaking humungous smile on my face. My virginity is finally gone!

Driving home from Zory's house tonight, I wish I had my dad to talk to. I know that I'll replay this for Oliver at some point, but not now. I don't want to do anything that will mess with his head. But this was a huge night for me. And I think that my dad would be proud that I waited to have sex until I was in love. From what my Mom tells me about him, he may have said something like, "Sex is much better when you care about the person you're with." And from my singular experience, I have to agree with him. I cannot imagine it being any better.

Oliver

I feel like I live in Megan's office. Dad drove me for the first session after I got out of the hospital, but I can now drive myself in a brand-new Toyota Corolla. It's a lame car, but it's black. I like that for some reason. I don't know what dad did with my mom's old car, but I know that he didn't want any reminders about my trying to kill myself. We talked about it a little at the hospital with the psychiatrist and with Megan last session. I get the feeling Dad wants to move on. That he cannot handle me being unstable and my mom being unstable at the same time. He made a choice and has placed his bet on me. This pisses me off. I share this with Megan, and she does that thing she always does when she wants me to figure shit out on my own: she puts her notebook aside, leans in, and doesn't say a fucking word.

"There's a lot of pressure for me to get my shit together."

Megan nods and almost smiles and doesn't feel the need to add anything to what I just said.

So I say, "And I don't know if I can get my shit together. My shit is fucking all over the place. Imagine having explosive diarrhea all over your office. And then some douchebag tells you that you have to gather it up and put it in a neat pile."

I know that I am intentionally being an asshole with this disgusting tirade, but Megan just keeps quiet and listens like I'm giving her the winning lottery numbers.

I continue, "It can *not* be done. There would be shit residue on your pretty white rug, probably on your couch, too. The shit will never, ever be together."

I lean back on Megan's couch and shut my mouth. She follows my lead and leans back on the white chair she always uses.

Finally, Megan says, "You are absolutely right. Trying to get your shit together always leaves stains. But these stains are reminders of the work you did to clean it up." Mic drop moment for Megan. She continues, "Nothing hard comes easy, and it's comforting to have reminders of that work."

When I get home that night, I think about our disgusting yet enlightening conversation. I believe Megan is correct, but what about shit that is all over the place in a room that no one goes in? That's what my brain feels like. It's a big, lonely place filled with thoughts I should not be thinking. Suddenly, a wave of guilt washes over me for not taking the meds that were prescribed for me when I was in the hospital. They will probably make my head feel better, but I feel both comfortable and agitated in the desolate room of my mind. I feel like it's kinda like home and that I don't want to leave that room because it's safe and everything outside that room is pointless. But while I'm in that room, I know that I will never get the shit cleaned up.

Kim

Thirteen days till Christmas and ten days until holiday break and it's all moving fast. Jules and I get home, and we immediately get to cookie baking. This is a tradition I started with Julia when she was five years old. It was much messier then, but she loved adding extra chips to the chocolate chip cookies and red and green sprinkles to the butter cookies. I always freehand the letters K, D, and J, and Julia is in charge of adding anything she wants to them. The three of us will eat our assigned cookies tonight after a gourmet dinner from Chipotle. Deven will grab our order on his way home from practice. I silently pray that this is a joyous dinner because I suspect he'll get his Princeton decision today. I've exercised a lot of self-control not to check. I know his username and password, but this is all him. He did the work, and he should be the one to know first.

Deven

I hurry out of practice and head to pick up dinner. When I get home, it smells like cookies, but I don't stop to snack on one. Dropping the Chipotle bags on the table, I yell to Mom, "I'm checking!" as I head up to my room. I open my laptop and pull up the Princeton admission page. I log in, and the website seems to take longer than usual to load.

I was deferred.

I want to throw my laptop across the room. I don't want my application to be lumped in with a million other applications.

Fuck!

I didn't realize that I'd shouted that out loud. And next thing I know, my mom is standing in my doorway, her eyes sad and her lips downturned.

"I am sorry, Deven," she says.

"I was deferred, Mom," I tell her, but I feel like I was rejected, so I hold up my hand just as she starts to say something. "And before you say something to try to make me feel better. Don't. I know everything you're going to say." And shockingly, Mom just nods. She walks over to me, rubs my back, kisses the top of my head, and leaves.

I pick up my phone and text Z.

deferred

Oh, Babe. I am sorry.
I know it's not what you want
but it's not a rejection

it feels like it

But you know it's not and that
Princeton is a long shot for everyone

I wish I hadn't told anyone

yeah. I get that.

I'll get over it

and maybe then you can
get under me 😏 🩶

I feel better already 🩶

I head downstairs, grab a Chipotle chip, and swipe a big glob of salsa on it. I put the whole thing in my mouth, and Julia starts to laugh. I smile, and so does Mom as she hands each of us our burritos. Jules tells us how a classmate fell asleep in class and the teacher stood over his desk and played the Old Phone ringtone on his phone. "You should have seen him," Julia giggles as she talks. "He was so freaked out that I think he may have peed his pants."

I manage to put the Princeton thing out of my mind for a few minutes and have fun with Mom and Jules. I keep thinking that this time next year, I'll be at college. And part of me is happy that I was deferred from Princeton because it gives me time to see where Zory is going to go.

Kim

As much as I hate shopping for myself, I love shopping for other peo-ple. But this year I'll be shopping for the man who has and seems to buy everything. I thought long and hard about this and plan to pur-chase a trip to Colorado for the two of us. Since he would have to give me some dates due to the patients he has scheduled, I'm going to wrap up some items to serve as clues. I already purchased fake snow, ski gloves, thermal socks, and a picture of Vail. I have not skied since Matthew and I went when Deven was two. My parents watched him, and we headed to the Poconos for a weekend. It was the last time we went away just the two of us.

My eyes fill with tears. Shit. I feel a meltdown coming on. I go upstairs to my bedroom so the kids don't see me, OP not far behind. I close the door and sit on the floor, leaning against it, and I cry, OP's head in my lap. Even now, I miss Matthew. I wonder what we would be like as a couple, as a family. I believe in my heart of hearts that we would be a tight unit. And of course, we would live through normal arguments or attitude from the kids. Matthew and I would take the kids to Phillies games and to the shore in the summer. Then again, this is all conjecture.

But this I know for sure: he would want me to move forward and be happy. I am at peace, and I do love Shawn, but it's a different kind of love. It's a grown-up love. Matthew and I had brand-new love, the love that changes a little and you grow into. But we didn't have the chance. Maybe that's what I really miss—the "what could have been."

I allow myself fifteen minutes of cry time and then take a long shower. After, I gently knock on Deven's door.

"Dev," I say after the knock. Deven opens his door, and I sit down at his desk, OP plopping down at my feet. Deven is across from me on his bed. He announces that he's fine before I can even ask a question.

"Maybe this was a good thing," he suggests.

"Maybe," I responded. "But I know that you will kick ass no matter where you go."

"Thanks, Mom."

I ask him if he has purchased anything for Zory for Christmas, and he says not yet. I tell him that he can borrow my credit card and spend up to $250 on a gift for her. His face brightens, and he hugs me and says that he knows exactly what he's going to buy her.

"Oh yeah? What's that?" I inquire.

Deven unlocks his phone and pulls up a picture of a very pretty and delicate bracelet. It would look lovely on Zory. It cost $249, so I add that I will also cover the tax. Deven thanks me profusely and hugs me again.

My mood is lighter as I head downstairs.

Julia

Girls Rule #8

So, Mr. J., It's Christmastime and every time I hear the song "The Twelve Days of Christmas," I think I really want a partridge in a pear tree. Not really! I hope I don't get THAT!!! I do not like birds or pears. But I do like Lululemon headbands. Here's what I bought everyone for Christmas. Mom—a Yankee Candle. Gram—same thing. Pop—a new Eagles ski cap. Deven—same thing. OP—a new tug toy. I got Allie a super cute top from Forever 21. That's all for now. I hope that you have a really good 12 days of Christmas.

Kim

It's December 23, and I am not ready for the onslaught of fun and festivities that will besiege my home within twenty-four hours. This past week, I was going to a holiday party every day. I went with Shawn to dinner with his staff at Butcher and Singer. I had forgotten how exquisite that restaurant is and how perfect their martinis are. Then he came with me to the Freedom party at Mandy's house. One of Oliver's teachers cornered him and went on about how Oliver has not been himself lately. We kept the suicide attempt as quiet as possible, but Zory and Sophia knew about it, so I have no idea who knows what. This faculty member apparently had zero clue about this or was just obnoxiously prying for information. Unfortunately, this particular teacher is one of the few at Freedom who are clueless and indiscreet.

But even with the holiday stress, I am in the Christmas spirit. And the birthday spirit. Did I mention that my birthday is December 26? Yes siree. Boxing Day and National Whiner's Day. Growing up, my parents never had a birthday cake on Christmas Day for me, even though we were with family and friends. My birthday was celebrated on my actual birth date. Everyone had to gather two days in a row, but no one really seemed to mind. My parents are excellent party hosts. I think that's why I enjoy hosting so much and exactly why I always have my mom's help. As this passes through the myriad holiday-related thoughts, my front door opens, and Mom appears, as if on cue.

She closes the door, pets OP, and walks to the kitchen. Mom shrugs off her parka and hugs me hard, and I hug back. We are a very huggie family. "Your dad is trying to find a place to park. The parking situation here is getting worse." And I wait for her to tell me again that I should move to the suburbs. She does not disappoint as she goes on to share a litany of reasons why I should relocate to Bucks County.

"I know," I concede. "But there are restaurants and bodegas within walking distance. Besides, I would never find a house with as much character as this one."

Mom gives a small smile in agreement, just as my dad comes in.

"Kimmie, Kimmie! This place looks amazing!" he exclaims as he pecks me on the cheek. I thank my dad and look around. The house certainly looks festive. I have a decorated tree in the living room's front window and one in the corner of the kitchen. Presents are placed under both trees, but I always put the family gifts under the tree in the window, a tradition that Matthew and I started when we purchased the house.

"Where are my grandkids?" Dad asks and I tell him that Jules is upstairs and should be down and that Deven is at Zory's house. "They're still hot and heavy?"

I laugh. "Dad! That is a cringe-worthy question. But yes. Deven is still with Zory." My dad chuckles and heads to the basement to get the supplies he needs. Matthew managed to collect many power tools, extension cords, and other random items from Lowes or Home Depot in his short life. I guess the engineer in him wanted to have all the necessary things on hand in the event of a home engineering emergency.

Mom and I get to work as Dad gets the sound system up and running. Christmas music will be playing on a loop from two o'clock in the afternoon tomorrow until the next morning.

Jules must hear her grandparents because she runs down and hugs them both. She sits on a stool in the kitchen as Mom and I make the baccalà salad. Baccalà is simply dried cod and is delicious. I purchased two dried cod and put them in trays of water. Most people put the trays in their refrigerator, but our basement is not heated and is cold enough

Anna Picari

in December to suffice. The water must be drained and replaced for two to three days so the cod is not super salty and is pliable.

"Gram, what snacks are we getting for New Year's Eve?" Julia blurts.

"Anything you want, Jules. I thought that you could come in the early afternoon, and we could go to the store," Mom answers. Julia is going to spend New Year's Eve with my parents because Shawn and I are going to dinner with his sister and brother-in-law.

"Yay! And we have to buy ingredients to make your world-famous brownies."

My mother tells Julia that they'll have time to make brownies and anything else that she wants as she's chopping up Kalamata olives and adding them to the cubed pieces of baccalà.

The rest of the fish will be purchased at Darigo's Fish Market, located in Philly's famous Ninth Street Italian Market, on Christmas Eve, and Kana and Dave will bring the "good bread" from Almonte's. The kids and I will wake up early, go to Starbucks, and head to the fish market. My parents will create a tray of homemade cookies and a tray of tiramisu for dessert.

We work for several hours, stopping only to order pizza delivery. Deven comes home just as my parents are leaving. They hug hello and goodbye, knowing they will see one another the next day.

Deven

I know this may sound lame, but Christmas Eve is my favorite holiday. It's really chill and no one is guarding the "grown-up" punch. I discovered this tasty beverage when I was thirteen. It's Mom's secret recipe, but it's cranberry juice, vodka, fresh lemons and limes, and some kind of sparkling wine. It's kind of strong, so I limit how much I pilfer. Tonight, though, Jules caught me, and later, I saw she had a cup in her hand that looked like punch. I have to keep an eye on her because Allie's with her.

Zory came over before the party started because her family was getting on a plane later that night to go to visit family in Nigeria. She had a wrapped bottle of something for Mom, who graciously accepted it and hugged Zory. "I am so grateful for you," she said. It looked like Mom was going to cry. Zory said thank you, and I pulled her upstairs so that she didn't have to face any more awkwardness.

I closed my door and pulled her into me. We stood there, kissing. I love her so much and still cannot believe that we're dating sometimes. When we broke apart, Zory opened her purse and handed me a card. "Open it," she commanded, and I obeyed.

It was a pop-out card of an elf holding mistletoe. The card read, *You are the only one I want under the mistletoe.* I laughed and tell her vice-versa. There was a smaller envelope, and I opened it to find a gift card for Tandem Skydiving, which made me smile because skydiving is something I have wanted to do for a long time, and I'll be eighteen soon and can go. Z will go too. I told her that it was perfect and then hurried to my desk and pulled out a perfectly wrapped (courtesy of Kim) gift. Z took a seat near the foot of my bed, and I sat in the middle and handed her the present.

"Wow. You did an awesome job wrapping," Zory said dubiously. And I admitted that it was obviously my mother's handiwork. She laughed knowingly and carefully unwrapped the gift. When she opened the lid of the box, she gasped and squealed and hugged me. "I love it, Deven. It's perfect. Put it on me!"

I was so happy to oblige, and the gold glimmered on her skin. It looked way more expensive than it was. Zory said she couldn't wait to show her parents and Sophia. I snapped a picture of her with it on it, and she posted it to IG almost immediately. We also took pictures together with both gifts, making sure to tag all the merchants, and posted them as well.

She left for the airport hours ago, and I'm just lying in my bed, listening to the party downstairs, drinking my holiday punch. I miss her already, but before I get too sad, Oliver comes into my room.

"Hey, man." I get up and we do that man-hug thing, and then we both just sit on the floor.

I hand him my punch, and he takes a slug and starts coughing. "There is a shit-ton of alcohol in this."

I just laugh, grab the cup back, and nod.

"Is Shawn here?" I ask, and Oliver tells me that Shawn had to check on a patient at the hospital first. Oliver walked over—one of the benefits of being neighbors on a night with very limited street parking. I suggest we head downstairs and get some grub.

"And more punch," Oliver adds from behind me.

Shawn shows up soon after and finds Oliver first. He gives him a hug and compliments what he's wearing, which causes me to notice what he has on: a pair of black jeans and a black pullover sweater. He looks good, so I tell him, though I note that there are no females at the party under the age of forty, with the exception of Julia and Allie. He laughs and says that maybe he would do better with a milf or a middle schooler. I punch his shoulder as we head in the direction of the food.

I make a stop at the punch bowl in the corner of the counter and pour two reasonably large cups. Just as I finish pouring, Pops speaks up from behind me. "Both for you?"

I jump a little, and then I laugh and tell him that one is for Oliver. Pops reminds me to watch him. Alcohol and depression don't mix. Sheesh. Everyone in my life is a therapist. I just nod and take off quickly to find Oliver, trying not to drop the overfilled cups.

"I saw the Insta posts with you and Z. That bracelet is fire. She must have loved it," Oliver says with sincere interest.

"Yeah. She loved it. And I can't wait to go skydiving with her," I add.

Oliver gives a small laugh and jokes, "I don't believe that anyone will be giving me a gift certificate to jump out of a plane. They'd be afraid I would intentionally forget the parachute."

I grab the letter that I wrote weeks ago and hand it to him. My mom gave it back to me when she realized that I put it with the other letters. I want him to understand that I need him here, in my life, and his comment about the plane was a weird thing to say, and it made me uncomfortable. But I also let him know that what he described is impossible because you're attached to an instructor when you tandem skydive. And then I change the subject to the upcoming Eagles game this weekend.

Kim

The party was in full swing. Everyone is laughing and chatting, and that makes my heart happy. I have been fighting a stomach thing since early this morning. I thought it was just nerves and excitement, but now I feel like it may be something I ate. As I sip my punch, I run through everything I ate in the last twenty-four hours and the only possible culprit is the pizza we ordered from Papa's Pizza yesterday when we were getting everything ready. Maybe the baccalà was bad. I hope not. It's always a fan favorite because it's a lighter dish and, quite frankly, very tasty and festive. The coffee at Starbucks this morning smelled weird and tasted worse. I wanted to send it back but would never do that when they were super busy with last-minute shoppers.

I push my nausea aside and decide to have a fun time. I look over and see Shawn yakking it up with my dad, and my heart swells. I think my parents really like Shawn and are making every effort to have a relationship with him. This comes easier for my mom, but my dad is not too bad either. My mom is sitting at the dining table between Kana and mom's sister, Barbara. She is my favorite aunt, and I have always been a little jealous of her fashion sense, always having shoes that match her bag or being able to buy a dress at TJ Maxx and making it look expensive. Aunt Barbara would never be caught anywhere in my sweaters. I pull up a chair and squeeze in between her and Kana.

Kana tells me that everything is fabulous, as usual, and Mom and I smile. Kana really likes food and thinks of herself as a connoisseur. She usually eats very mindfully but, looking at the two empty martini glasses next to her plate, I think perhaps mindful eating went out the window an hour ago. But I don't care. I love her, my friend of a lifetime. She can eat the lobster as fast as she wants. She's earned that.

"What, don't you have a plate?" Kana asks, and I tell her that I think I ate something that hit me the wrong way. "Well, let's get you a fizzy water." And Kana gets up, wobbles a little, and heads to grab a Perrier.

By the time Kana gets back, my mom is chatting up a storm with her sister, and I'm just sitting there eating some oyster crackers that were on the table.

"Here. Drink this," Kana demands, so I do. And I continue to munch on the crackers. Kana picks up her third martini glass, takes a slug, looks at me, and then her face gets a weird expression. She pulls me close to her and whispers, "Let's go to your room."

I am only a smidge tipsy from the punch, but I laugh and say, "I always knew you wanted me. You know, in a sexual way."

"Yes. And even more if you wear one of your long, drab sweaters."

"Hey! That's not nice. I'm always cold," I whine, but I get up, and Kana and I walk upstairs to my bedroom. Kana closes the door, and she pulls me onto the bed next to her.

"You're pregnant!" she blurts out.

It takes a minute for her words to register, but I shake my head. No, not possible. And I start to laugh.

"So you're telling me that you never, ever had unprotected sex with Shawn?"

I think about this and then freeze. I have no response.

"I *knew* it!" Kana says.

I say nothing because I'm thinking.

"Well?" she presses.

"Jesus, I'm thinking. Not to sound like an a-hole, Kana, but we have a lot of sex."

Anna Picari

And as soon as I say it, I remember. I don't think we used protection the day Shawn stopped home to get some items for Oliver when he was in the hospital. But that was less than four weeks ago. Would I be having symptoms yet? The wheels in my head are turning now. I had some spotting a few weeks ago, but I just thought it was perimenopause. My mom was finished with her period before she turned forty-six, so I just thought the light period was indicative of my moving into perimenopause. And I say as much.

Kana thinks about this for a minute and replies, "You may be right but that wouldn't explain the nausea or fatigue."

"What fatigue?'

"Oh, I don't know if you're fatigued, but you have been looking exhausted for weeks. No offense. I just thought it was the holidays." Kana lies back onto my bed, but not before snatching the half full cup out of my hand, raising it to her lips, and finishing it.

When she finishes swallowing, she says, "You need to take a pregnancy test."

I jump off the bed, reach down, and grab Kana's hand. Pulling her up, I say, "We need to get to the party. I'm sure that my mother is wondering where I am."

Kim

Not long after my alarm goes off at 6:00 a.m., I wish Matthew a Merry Christmas and blow a kiss up to the ceiling. I'm feeling at peace because I believe in my heart of hearts that Matthew would approve of my relationship. Shawn treats me well and gets along with Deven and Jules.

But I'm glad that Shawn went home last night with Oliver so that I have these moments to thank God for the blessing of having had two amazing men care for me, and for Oliver, who seemed like he had a good time. It made my heart swell with happiness to see him smile and laugh. I also know that this could be a sign that Oliver has made another plan and is comfortable implementing it. But some research says that this is not always true. The one thing that *is* true is that we're not out of the woods with Oliver yet. He needs at least a year of intensive therapy and probably some group work.

Scootching up and leaning on the headboard, I do a quick mental rundown of all that needs to be done. I am wearing my red flannel pajamas, and I grab my Mickey Mouse Santa hat with *Kimmie* written in silver letters across the white rim. I head downstairs.

After starting the coffee, I make sure everything is ready. The gifts are under the tree, and I get the french toast breakfast casserole out of the fridge to get it to room temperature before baking it.

The house always smells wonderful while it's baking and is another Orsetti Christmas tradition. My mom is bringing the already-cooked bacon at seven-thirty because the kids usually get up around eight. I'm sure Julia will sleep late because I caught her sipping some of the punch with Allie, who I have really grown to like a lot. She has calmed down a bit and has been a good friend to Jules.

I pour myself a cup of coffee and open the back patio door to let OP out. He's wearing a neck bandana with Christmas trees on it, and he looks so freaking cute. After he finishes his business and is back inside, I give him a treat and invite him to sit next to me on the couch. Like usual, he curls right next to me, and I instinctively pet him. I look down at his reddish-grayish coat. I pull his little face up so that he's looking directly at me, and I say, "You have saved my life over and over. You are the best dog in the world, and I love you so, so much." And I start to cry. What the fuck is happening? Is Kana right? Am I pregnant?

There has to be a store open, but I don't want anyone asking questions about where I'm going, so I'll just leave it for now.

But maybe I'll get a bonus birthday present tomorrow.

I take a huge sip of my coffee and then wonder if I should be drinking coffee or if I'm even happy about the possibility of having a baby. I will be forty-three tomorrow, and the risks of genetic abnormalities are high. I guess I will make a decision about this once I know for sure. But having another child was never on my mental radar. I have my two, crazy-perfect kids and they're enough for me.

Looking down at OP, I know that I would love to have a second dog, but I never seem to have the time. And I know that however great that second dog would be, he would not be as great as Optimus Prime, the dog to shame all dogs. And would that be fair to him?

My parents let themselves in and hang up their coats in the coat closet. I hug them both and say Merry Christmas. Mom left the presents for the kids yesterday, so all she had to unload was the bacon. I preheat the oven and ask Mom if she wants some coffee. She says no, but she's looking at me in a weird way. "Are you okay, Kimmie?"

I debate whether to let my mom in on my situation. And I quickly decide not to say anything. What if I'm not pregnant, and just old? What if there's something wrong with the baby? Would I terminate? I believe that women should have one hundred percent autonomy over their bodies, but I never had to think about what I would decide because I have only gotten pregnant intentionally. Well, I guess that only holds water if I'm not pregnant.

Forty-fucking-three! If I'm pregnant, I'll be sixty-one when this kid graduates from high school. My mom is a very young sixty-seven, but I don't know if she could handle a teenager.

So I choose to say, "I'm great, Mom. Just tired from last night."

She takes that and runs with it.

". . . everyone had such a good time . . . the food was outstanding. We outdid ourselves . . . it was nice that the neighbors were able to stop by this year." And on and on.

I am grateful for the subject change.

The morning progresses as usual, except Shawn and Oliver come over for breakfast. But they don't stay long. They're heading to visit Aubrey at the halfway house for Christmas dinner. The women there are all going to cook a huge feast and exchange small gifts. Shawn told me that Oliver got a few thoughtful gifts for Aubrey and was excited to give them to her. As they're getting ready to leave, Shawn pulls me into a big hug and says, "See you tomorrow, birthday girl," and I laugh and hug him back. He smells so good.

My parents, the kids, and I just hang out after all the presents are opened. Julia makes sure to get pictures of my mom and me with our matching candles and dad and Deven wearing their new Eagles hats with her new iPhone. I also made sure she got a strong case cover. That girl drops a lot of things. I took our annual picture of Deven, Julia, and OP in front of the tree. These are always my favorite pictures. What will the picture look like next Christmas?

　　　　　　　　　　　　　　　　　　　Anna Picari

Oliver

It's the day after Christmas, and I'm heading to Megan's office. I swear that woman never takes a day off. I have no desire to rehash the events of the last week. My appointment is at 11:00 a.m., and I'm early, so I stopped by Wawa to get a Gatorade. I think about getting Megan a coffee. Does she drink coffee? I have no idea what's in her purple Stanley cup. I decided to get her a hot chocolate. Everyone likes that, right?

At eleven on the dot, Megan opens her door and lets me in. I hand her the hot chocolate. "I got you some hot chocolate." She thanks me and motions for me to sit on the couch.

I never know what to do on that couch. There's a fluffy blanket off to one side. Would it be weird if I lay down? Not that I am going to do that! We would have had to discuss my new position, and I really don't want to talk about anything.

"So, Oliver. How was Christmas?" Megan starts, and I just shrug. "What does the shrug mean? I only took basic shrugging in college." She knew that this would get me to smile. I like when she tries to be funny.

I explained that it was pretty good, and I was happy to see my mom. The food that the women at the halfway house cooked was really good and interestingly eclectic. Everything from honey-baked ham to cornbread to collard greens to homemade mac and cheese. My mom was in charge of appetizers and made two huge trays of loaded nachos, complete with beef, cheese, jalapeños, shredded chicken, and refried beans. I told Megan that they had a ton of food and every nonalcoholic beverage known to humankind.

"It sounds like a nice party," Megan comments, and I agree with her. She sits back on her chair and takes a long sip on her hot chocolate. Should I have gotten whipped cream? She seems too serious to like whipped cream. Sometimes, I think she just likes to find different ways to make me uncomfortable so that I have to wait and eventually say something. But today I want to make her wait, like we're playing therapy chicken. But she sees what I'm doing and gets comfortable in her chair, crosses her legs, and takes another sip of hot chocolate. Finally, I break.

"What did you do for the holiday?" I ask jovially.

"Why is it important for you to know what I did?"

"Oh. Come. *On!* I'm just being polite. I really don't give a fuck what you did. Happy now?" I snarl.

Megan takes a deep breath and exhales in this dramatic way that she always does. "Having any suicidal ideation?" Megan blurts out.

I feel like I was slapped for a second and have to think about what I am going to say.

"Suicidal ideation? Umm. No." Yeah. I am thinking about offing myself every minute of every day, although now I feel a little better because I think I have a really good idea.

"Suicidal plans?" Megan quickly responds, and I shake my head. "Use your words, Oliver."

"No, Megan. I have no plan." Which is a total lie because I absolutely have a plan. But I'd rather be dead than sent to a mental hospital. She lets out a sigh of relief and says something positive. But she's always saying something positive. I wish that positivity was contagious because maybe then I would not be living in this hellhole of my mind all the time.

"Okay but remember our deal. It still stands. You call me if you ever feel the urge to hurt yourself. You have my personal cell phone number and my special office number. If, for some reason, I do not answer, call 911. I am trusting you because I believe that we have an honest and true working relationship."

And now I just feel like total shit. I really like Megan, but she doesn't grasp the pain and hopelessness and feeling of being a vast container of nothingness. And I tried to explain it to her, and she says that she understands, but she can't possibly because if she truly understood, she would have made plans to end her own life.

I feel like an asshole because I don't really have an answer for her. I wish I could say that I'm all better because things in my life are better but it's not working that way. I am aware that my dad is happy and my mom is doing better. I know that I was an a-hole to Sophia and am happy to be her friend, but I cannot fucking shake this feeling. This nonstop, whispering-in-my-ear feeling that I am never going to feel better. The emptiness of hopelessness has taken up a prime parking space in my brain.

Deven

I miss Zory more than I have ever missed anyone. That's a shitty thing to think since I lost my dad. My mom told me that I was so sad when he died and that I used to wait by the front window for hours for him to come home. But to be honest, I have no recollection of it. Maybe it was so sad that I repressed the memory, and maybe one day I will have hypnosis or something to help bring back the trauma that I apparently suffered. But in a weird way, I miss him now. I feel like I have so many things that I need to talk to a man about. For instance, I like the way a guy looks with just a hint of beard. When I try it, I look like I just didn't care enough to shave for a few days. I have Google, but I learn better by observation and there is no one here to observe.

Back to Z. Is it wrong that I want to go to college with her? Mom thinks that it's unfair because Zory deserves to be out and about, meeting new people without me in the shadows. She makes me sound like a creeper, but maybe she's right. I'm afraid for Zory to meet new people because she may find people that she likes more than me. I know this is a very selfish point of view, but I love her so much, and the thought of us not being together makes me want to throw up. Just thinking about it! But there are all kinds of stories on TikTok about high school couples who break up at college and then get back together in their late twenties, so I think of this as my backup plan. Even if she meets some frat douchebag, he will never be as good as me.

As everyone in our family circle is aware, today is Mom's birthday. I have to say, she is a great mom. She gets on my nerves sometimes, but that has to be normal. Gram and Pops are taking us to dinner tonight. I think Shawn feels left out because they took over the b-day plans. He's got to understand that this is just how we've been doing it. They haven't even been dating for a year, and he is at least invited. So is Oliver. Mom gets to pick the restaurant, and I think we're heading to Buddakan. I love that place. The food is Asian fusion, and I have never eaten anything there that was not delicious. We normally get a lot of plates to share, and I hope that Shawn does not mess this up for us.

Kim

My birthday dinner was lovely. We had a table for eight, even though there were only seven of us, and we ate and laughed and ate some more. My stomach was not bothering me today, so I put the pregnancy thing out of my mind. However, just to be on the safe side, I only had two glasses of Pinot Grigio. I probably shouldn't have had even that, but I am relatively confident that I am not pregnant, and that was Kana being dramatic. And I told her so when we met for lunch today. We always have such a good time, laughing and telling stupid stories. I'm lucky to have her in my life. She's like my sister, and I think she feels the same way about me.

Today, I'm going to straighten the house out. It looks as if a tornado went through the downstairs, and the mess makes me anxious. Shawn said that he'll coming over to keep me company, but honestly, I'd rather have him help me clean.

Is it too soon for me to ask that of him?

Matt and I moved in together rather quickly, so we always helped each other, whether it was painting the shutters or mopping the kitchen floor. Maybe Shawn doesn't think about cleaning because he has a cleaning service that comes to his house twice a week. I believe that is excessive, but Shawn likes this company because they create and pack healthy lunches for him to grab for work. We may have to keep that part of their service if we ever move in together because I bring a banana and a whole jar of almond butter with me to work and that suffices as my lunch on most days. On Fridays, the office staff, who gratefully always include me, pick a local restaurant and take orders. By Friday, it's a godsend because I'm totally sick of bananas and almond butter. I repeat it every week, but sometimes, I substitute carrots and hummus for the banana and peanut butter. At work, I just need easy sustenance to keep me moving throughout my day. I am not one to be packing lunch for a man. I don't even pack my kids' lunches anymore. By the time the kids were in fifth grade, they were expected to pack their own lunches. And it has worked out pretty well. I allow them to purchase lunch at school once a week, but the other days, they can pull whatever they feel like and put it in their lunch boxes.

I went home with Shawn after my birthday dinner last night because I knew that Deven would be home with Julia and Oliver was coming over to play video games. It was the first time that we were alone in at least a week, and I cherished the quiet time together. I was wearing the diamond necklace that he purchased for me for Christmas. It is lovely, and I like that it has a very sturdy chain so that I don't have to take it off. Shawn really liked the idea of going skiing together, and he thinks that he can get away at the very end of February. I will book everything after the New Year when his office staff are all back from Christmas vacation.

Julia

Girls Rule #9

Dr. J, What's up???? Lol. You are not Dr J, but again, I try to do weird things with your last name. And before you say a word . . . Of course, I know who Julius Erving is. I was born and raised in Philly. Ha!!! I always wanted to say that, but I would never say that out loud. I would sound like a weirdo. I get the feeling that my classmates don't like Philadelphia like I do. Want to know what is going on? Well, Christmas was amazing. And Mom's birthday was a few days ago. We always have a lot of fun when we go out for that, but this year, Mom invited Shawn and Oliver. It was okay, I guess, but I like it just being us. Oliver is over now with Deven. Mom is with Shawn. Tomorrow is New Year's Eve, and I am going to spend it with Gram and Pop. We always have fun. I'll sleep with Gram, and Pop will sleep in the guest room. But we will stay up until midnight, and we can see the fireworks from their back patio. They are the best grandparents in the world. But right now, I am bored, and that is a bad thing for me to be, so I am going to text some of my friends from school. Allie and I have been sitting with Holly, Amica, and Samantha at lunch, and we hang when we have classes together. We have a group snap, and it's really fun. I still like Allie the best, but I also like being part of a group. Do you know what I mean?

Oliver

Today's the day. I told Deven I was going to meet up with him and the guys at Connor's house at eight thirty, but I won't be able to make their little soiree. Lying on my bed, I consider writing new notes. I know that Deven read his because he told me when he gave me the response letter at Christmas. When I got home on Christmas Eve, I read the letter again and cried. And then I ripped up the letter because I know what I know, and I know that he loves me. I know that my parents love me, but it's not enough to make this emptiness go away. I think I may just write a generic note, trying to explain my reasons. I grab a piece of paper and pen.

Dear People I Love,

This is not your fault. I know that you love me so much. I love you just as much, but I cannot stay alive anymore. The pain that is with me is like a black hole that keeps wanting to suck me in. It fills my mind with feelings of emptiness, and I feel that any effort to get away from these feelings is futile. I have tried. Believe me. I have felt this way for almost two years. I did a pretty good job acting like everything was great in the beginning. But it hasn't been great, or even good, for a while. I am trying to help you understand what is going on, but I feel like I am failing, so think of it this way. . . . It's like from the minute I open my eyes in the morning until I close them at night, I feel so mentally weak that I cannot even remember my name. To ask me to try to do the smallest task takes more energy that I am capable of. That is why I have been such a dick. I am angry at myself for not being able to get out of this hell. I am sorry that I have been a dick to you. You do not deserve this.

Dad, take care of Deven and Kim (and even Jules) for me. They are special people, and I know that they will be sure to take care of you. And be sure to check in on Mom from time to time.

Mom, stay clean. Maybe find a career that you love. Make new friends and have an amazing life. When I was little, I always told you that you were the most beautiful person in the whole world. I still think that. You are so kind and have a big smile. Thank you for giving me your smile.

I am doing this today so that tomorrow you can start anew. This year, this day will suck but you have the better and newer tomorrow to look forward to.

I will be watching over all of you, I promise. Tell Deven that whenever he sees someone in Wawa with a baseball cap on sideways, that is the signal that I am watching him. He'll know what this means.

I love you. I hope that next year brings you happiness and joy. You all deserve it.

Love Forever and Ever,

Oliver

Satisfied with the letter and praying that it helps a little, I fold it and kiss the front of it. I write: *To Everyone That I Love.*

I hear Dad in the kitchen, and I look at the clock and it says 5:05. I need to be at the spot by just after 6:00. I head out and see that he's already dressed to go out. He's a handsome guy, I think. Is it weird to think that about your dad?

"Are you looking for something?" I ask.

"Yes. I cannot find my good reading glasses," he responds, and I look in the den. He sometimes reads things on his iPad there. I move one of the pillows and voila!

"I found them," I shout as Dad makes his way into the room. I hand them over, and he smiles and says thank you. "No problem, I say." I then tell him that he looks really good and that Kim will be all over him. He just rolls his eyes and asks if I need anything. I lie and tell him that we're all sleeping at Connor's, and he's supplying everything. Just before he leaves, I hug him and say, "Happy New Year, Dad. I love you."

He pulls away and looks me in the eye and says, "Happy New Year, Oliver. I love you too. So very much. And I am so proud of you."

I hug him again so that he doesn't see the tears in my eyes because I feel like such a fucking dick right now. He gives a little wave and heads to the garage to get the Tesla.

After he leaves, I check my phone and see there's a text from Deven.

want to hang here before the party?

can't. I need to get in the shower and shit

Oh. okay. see you at C's house.

yep see you soon.

I straighten up my room, make my bed, and leave the note in the middle on my pillow. I put my wallet on my nightstand. I head to the front door once I know my dad is gone, I shut the door behind me, and get in my car.

Kim

Well, I picked up a pregnancy test on my way home from dropping Jules off at my parents' house. I figured I would tell Shawn at midnight if I was and would drink a lot if I wasn't. It's weird, but I'm starting to hope that I am pregnant.

I love being a mom, and I think I'm pretty good at it. I have never raised a child with anyone, though. I mean, Deven was four when Matt died, so we didn't have a lot of opportunity to coparent. If I had this baby, Shawn and I would raise him or her together. Hmmmm . . . I think Shawn is a pretty good dad, but the fact that he was gone for long periods of Oliver's childhood due to his job kept him from doing a lot of the things that dads are supposed to do. I guess I have that covered, too, if need be. Good thing I have practice being both parents.

I head up to my room, undress, and get in the shower. I wrap a towel around myself, sit on the toilet, and unwrap the first of the two pregnancy tests that are in the box. I take the cap off and pee on the stick. I place it on the vanity and finish peeing. I won't look at it for the full three minutes that the instructions say to wait. I finished toweling off and put on my new black bra and panties, which were a birthday present from Kana. I go back to the bathroom to grab my makeup bag and look down at the stick and see the word: Pregnant. I quickly open the second Clearblue that was in the box and manage to get a few drops of urine on that one as well. I don't have to wait three minutes; the word appears almost immediately.

Holy fuck!

I find my phone on my nightstand charging and call Kana.

"Hey," Kana answered jovially.

"I'm pregnant!" I say with a very nervous edge to my voice.

"Oh wow! I love being right."

"Very funny, Kana, but now I will be worried about all the things that can go wrong with advanced maternal age. How did this happen? My eggs have got to be shit, right?"

"Well, the one that caught the sperm seems like it was okay. Are you going to tell Shawn, or are you going to wait until you talk to an OB?" Kana wants to know.

"I'm going to tell Shawn at midnight. We can start the new year bonded together by this possibility. Do you think I shouldn't tell him yet? No, I have to tell him. Right?"

"Kim, relax. You do whatever you want, whenever you want. I'll support any decision you make." Kana is always the voice of reason.

"Okay. I've got to finish getting dressed. I promise I'll call you to-morrow. I love you."

"Ditto!" Kana responds and hangs up.

I put on my makeup with shaky hands and pull my hair into a high ponytail. I spray the sides so that it's more sleek than casual. I carefully pull a black cashmere sweater over my head, put on my black slacks, and slip into Sam Edelman flats. Just as I reach down the front of my sweater to pull the necklace out, there's a knock on the front door. As I walk downstairs, I make a mental note to remind him again to use the keypad. He has the code.

Shawn greets me with a big hug as he tells me I look "hot." I laugh and tell him that he looks hot as well and that we'll be the hottest cou-ple at the restaurant. I ask him if he wants a glass of wine since we have some time before we have to be at the restaurant.

"Sure. I'll get it," Shawn says as I sit at the counter. I watch as he pulls two wine glasses down from the cabinet and expertly opens the bottle with the wine opener. Shawn has an elegance to him, and I appreciate this, I think. He places a glass in front of me and we clink.

"To a new year," Shawn says.

"To a new beginning," I add, thinking about the life growing inside me. I take a small sip, put my glass down, and kiss him deeply. "I love you, Shawn."

"I love you, too, my Kim."

Oliver

A sense of comfort and weightlessness overcomes me as I drive to the bridge. I see signs for historical landmarks, like the Liberty Bell and the Edgar Allan Poe House, as I make my way to I-676. It's 6:08, and as I take the exit off of I-76 for the Walt Whitman Bridge, I can see the fireworks display from the Waterfront. They're beautiful. One of the reasons I picked New Year's Eve at this time is because of the fireworks. I'm not a dramatic guy, but who wouldn't want to finish it off in a big way? The city intentionally shoots them off at 6:00 p.m. on New Year's Eve so that little kids can see them. I think this is a very cool thing for the city to do.

I know I have to move quickly because there's no shoulder on this massive bridge. I stop in the middle of the road, keeping the car running and turning on my flashers. I don't want anyone to get hurt. I'm standing outside my car watching the fireworks when the phone rings, and my car's Bluetooth announces, "Call from D-dog."

Deven.

Epilogue

Kim

The front door opens, and I hear, "Mom, I'm here. Not really awake but here."

Jules.

I hurry downstairs and greet my girl. I wrap my arms around and squeeze the shit out of her like I haven't seen her in years, when in fact, it's only been a week.

Julia is studying English Literature at Villanova University (Go, Wildcats!). I have ceased asking her what she plans to do with that particular degree because she usually says something snarky, like "the universe will lead me." *Translation: Stop asking. I have no idea. I will be moving back with you and working at Starbucks.* But I keep my mouth shut. Usually.

Julia is a typical college student. She has a large group of friends, a carryover from her high school days. Middle school is generally the worst time for kids, but somehow, Julia blossomed and became one hundred percent herself. She and Allie, who went to technical school during high school and became a hair stylist, are still friends today and get together often. Immersing herself in clubs and student government, Julia found her voice and now uses it on her college campus. She's active in local politics and writes an editorial blog.

"Is Deven here yet?" Julia asks.

"Not yet. He just called. He's stuck in traffic. He'll be here in ten minutes."

Jules just grunts and complains, "What the hell, Mom? You called me at 6 a.m. to make sure that I got here on time."

I hand her a cup of coffee and remind her that she has specific challenges when it comes to being on time. Just then, the back door opens, and Rocky, our five-year-old Labradoodle, rushes in, my parents not far behind. After the best dog that ever lived passed away six years ago, we "adopted" Rocky from a breeder in our neighborhood. With a chocolate brown coat with a patch of white on his chest and pretty, greenish-colored eyes, he was clearly the cutest puppy in the litter. And fortunately for us, he is calm and lovable. OP would approve. We decided to name him after Rocky Balboa, the infamous and fictitious character who iconically charged up the Philadelphia Art Museum's stairs with arms outstretched in a winning fashion. We had just decided to move out of the city to give all of us a change of scenery and begin our next chapter when we met him. The dog's name paid homage to the city that will always be my hometown. You can take the girl out of Philly, but you can't take Philly out of the girl.

"Kim, the dog has been barking for five minutes. Glad you don't have any neighbors," my mom chides. She's being facetious because *she* is my neighbor. That is, she and my dad are. We purchased a home on a fourteen-acre lot in Pipersville, Pennsylvania, and made a guest cottage out of the barn that was on the property. I am grateful to have them with me, and they're both loving living in "the country," as they call it. Mom has planted a beautiful garden in front of the main house and her cottage. In late spring, her annuals would even make Martha Stewart proud. She wants to get a few chickens, and I am about to relent. There's nothing like fresh eggs. Dad loves driving his new ride-on mower, which doubles as a snowplow in winter, as well as helping Shawn and Deven string Christmas lights around the entire house. It's comical to watch three perfectionists navigate a hundred strings of lights.

I am lost in my thoughts as I hear Deven come in, greeted immediately by Rocky and then his sister. He greets everyone and then asks me, "Where is the future scholar?"

                                                        Anna Picari

On cue, I hear Shawn coming downstairs. He announces, "Ladies and gentlemen, put your hands together for our new first-grade superstar: Mattie Angela Orsetti-McDaniel!" (Mattie was chosen to honor Matthew, and Angela was chosen because it's my mom's first name.) Mattie descends with her princess crown on her head, her uniform pressed and stiff-looking, smiling wide. That girl loves an audience.

She's on the small side for her age due to being born at thirty-one weeks, but what she lacks in stature, she makes up for in personality. We gather around her and make a fuss, and she twirls and shows everyone her new backpack and lunch box, talking a mile a minute. I contemplate whether I'll have the energy to nag her about majoring in theater when I am in my sixties.

Just as she sits down to eat her cereal, Mattie stops chattering and asks, "Where's Oliver?"

Shawn replies, "I'm so sorry, baby. His plane was delayed, and he won't be able to be here this morning. But he told me to tell you that he will absolutely be here when you get home." This seems to appease her.

"It's okay. I will tell him all about it after school," Mattie concedes.

I announce that it's time to meet the bus, and we head out the front door, where the decorated golf cart awaits. One of the beautiful things about living on an oversized lot (with six bedrooms and five baths) is that the bus comes directly to your driveway, which, in our case, sometimes requires a golf cart if we're in a hurry.

Mattie sits in the back, facing outward, as Shawn and I get in the front. She waves to her adoring fans and shouts, "I'll see you later. Wish me luck."

And Julia, Deven, and my parents call positive affirmations at her.

I laugh when I hear Jules shout, "Be yourself, Mattie, but not too much!"

After ensuring that Mattie was safely on the bus, Shawn heads to his office. His practice is still in Philadelphia, but he only works four days—three in the office and surgery on the fourth day. He says he doesn't mind the fifty-minute drive because our new compound (as he calls it) is wonderful to come home to. Deven and Julia stay for the pancakes that my mom is making and then head off to their lives, promising they will be back for dinner. Julia heads to her 9:00 a.m. class, and Deven heads to work. He's an electrical engineer at a new firm in Doylestown. His apartment, which he shares with his girlfriend of two years, Clare, is in Lahaska. They met while in college at Princeton and had an instant connection. She is a pediatric nurse who is simply lovely and lively. Her personality fits right in.

I left Freedom when we moved to Pipersville. It was such a hard decision, but I felt that with a new baby, it was the right time. I opened a private practice in Doylestown so that I would have an excuse to stalk my son at work. Just kidding. I picked the location because of the location. It's central to many smaller towns. My practice gives me flexibility to be a homeroom mom for Mattie's class at Our Lady of Guadalupe and be home when Shawn has his day off. Rocky comes with me to the office and provides added support for my clients. He is so gentle with them, and it's as if he knows that they are hurt or healing and need unconditional love.

Oliver lives in Florida. After the bridge incident and copious amounts of counseling, he decided he needed a change. He sent in a late application to the University of Central Florida, where he received his bachelor's, and four years later, he applied to Florida State University, where he's currently working on his PhD in Clinical Psychology. He interns at a practice that specializes in working with teenagers. We don't see him as much as we see Deven and Julia, but he flies up as often as he can. And we have been to Florida a lot. We secretly hope that he moves back when he finishes, but I have a feeling that he's turning into a Floridian. He has nice friends and has alluded to a boyfriend. Oliver came out to us when he was nineteen, and we were all supportive, of course—even my dad and mom, who have become his grandparents through marriage. And apparently, he told Sophia that he sometimes felt attracted to boys while they were in high school. Oliver will share any relationship news when he feels it's appropriate.

When I think about Oliver, my heart swells with pride and love. He is the bravest and most resilient person I have ever met.

                                                      Anna Picari

Oliver

I'm sitting in the Jacksonville International Airport after the almost three-hour drive from Tallahassee. I park myself at the bar in Shula's airport hub. I order an old-fashioned, neat, and smile at the bartender. He's really cute and returns the smile.

I say, "Hey, hottie. Want to come to Philly with me?" He tells me that he doesn't go home with customers. "Thank God," I say, and he laughs. He's my boyfriend, Noah. Noah works here to help pay off his student debt and does marketing during the day for a start-up. He's a goal-oriented person, and I am people-oriented. And we just work. We met two years ago at FSU's Relay for Life cancer fundraiser. I was volunteering, and he, an FSU alum, was a runner. Noah ran into me as I was handing out water during Mile 7 of the race. He was in the zone and didn't see my arm, which caused the water to go everywhere. He looked back as he continued the run and smiled at me. And I am happy that he looked for me after the race.

I let him work while I sip my strong drink—another positive to having a bartender boyfriend. I reminisce whenever I'm heading back to Pennsylvania about the journey that took me to hell and back and to hell again, as my mom says, because I ended up in Florida. I love her when she dumps on Florida and often uses a quote that was used by John Oliver in an episode of *Last Week Tonight*: "Just because Florida is shaped like a dick doesn't mean they have to act like one." I like that one, too, and I know that Florida is a governmentally conservative state, but the people I've met are not. They are either middle of the road or lean left. They want change in the state government but don't know what they can do other than use their right to vote. I sometimes think about moving back to Pennsylvania to be closer to my family, but I don't know yet. I like really being on my own.

Well, kind of on my own. My dad and Kim, with a little help from my mom, are paying for school, room, and board. Gram and Pops (they make me call them that, but I like it) give me money all the time. Gram actually uses both Zelle and Venmo. And I miss Deven and Jules and definitely Mattie. That angel came into my life at a time when I needed something new and good. I love my little sister more than any-one. We have a special bond, and I Facetime her on her iPad every day.

Taking a long draw on my drink, my mind wanders back to that New Year's Eve. I was stuck in a depression so heavy that I felt like my days were like quicksand; at any time, I would be sucked down into a hole. The daily pain of that sadness and the feeling that my life was hopeless, that I would never get better, had me moving through my days like a ghost. I was not really there, and my insides felt transparent.

I was going to do it. I was ready and at peace. The fireworks were blasting and beautiful. As I stopped on the bridge, I noticed a few other cars had stopped for a perfect view of the celebratory fireworks, and I worried that the Delaware River Port Authority Police would shoo us away. I had so much change and rocks in my pockets and my shoes that it must have added ten pounds to my body. I was determined to get it right.

After I parked the still-running car, I got out and stood there for a minute, the car door was still open just as I was moving closer to the rail. And then my phone rang, and my car's Bluetooth announced a call from D-dog. Deven. I hesitated. I wanted to die. I needed not to be in the world anymore so my pain would go away. The phone stopped ringing, and I breathed a sigh of relief. But five seconds later, I heard again, "Call from D-dog. Answer it?" I remember being pissed off at Deven. At his persistence, I decided I would answer it and lie and then get back to what I was doing.

                                        Anna Picari

I said, "Hey, Dev. What's going on?"

"Oh, good. Hey. I was worried about you."

I took a deep breath and said, "What are you worried about, you freak?"

And Deven went on to tell me that he had a feeling that I was going to do something to myself and that if I did, he would never forgive himself.

"Where are you, Oliver?" he asked pointedly.

"Ummm, nowhere big," I responded in a lame and not-so-clever voice.

"I hear fireworks that are really loud. Are you on the river somewhere?"

Glad I didn't have to add another lie to the many that I had told, I said, "Yeah. They are very cool."

"Tell me exactly where you are. I'll meet you and watch, too," Deven pressed.

I remember the guilt that I felt having to lie to my best friend again. And I thought about the pain he would have to live with because of this. And I finally said, "I'm on the WWB." And I heard what sounded like a gasp from Deven.

"Well, I am about two minutes from there," Deven lied. "I've been driving around, looking for you. You weren't at your house, so I called Connor, and he said you weren't there yet. So I was just looking at the usual places, and then when I stopped to check at Wawa, I saw this a-hole with his hat on sideways and just had to try to call you again."

Deven later told me that he headed straight to the bridge once he heard the fireworks mixed with the cars passing by, but he wasn't sure which one to choose. He threw the mental dice because his thoughts were between either the Ben Franklin or the Walt Whitman. He decided on the WWB because it doesn't have the train that runs on it. At the time, I was impressed by that fucker's deductive reasoning.

Suffice it to say, Deven pulled behind me on the bridge as I was leaning on the railing, fireworks blazing. He parked behind me, flashers on.

"Oh my God, Oliver. Oh my God." Deven was crying and hugging me and crying and hugging me.

Before I knew what was happening, my dad's car was behind Deven's. He stopped his space machine and got out of the car as fast as the Tesla would let him. He ran up to us and hugged us both. Then Kim materialized and joined the really uncomfortable hug-fest.

"We need to get off this bridge before a Port Authority Cop gets here. They have cameras, you know," Kim said matter-of-factly. "I'll drive Oliver's car. Oliver, go with your dad. Let's go to your house, Shawn."

And with that directive, plan number two had been thwarted. I got into Dad's car, leaned back in the leathery seat, and cried. I remember only crying and apologizing and crying and apologizing, with my dad saying, "It will be alright, Ol," over and over in response to my apologies.

I went into residential treatment on January 3 at the Mayo Clinic in Minnesota. January 1 and 2 were a lot of fun with my dad chained to me. He even slept with me until we got on that plane. But the program in Minnesota was the turning point for me. I was away for thirty days, but my parents and Kim flew out twice to see me. I was in class every day and worked hard in my classes. They were a good distraction, if I'm being honest. I resumed regular school when I got back and went to my counselor to discuss college options.

I explained that I had the Temple and Drexel applications done, but I wondered if there were any schools out of state that I would like. She mentioned that Freedom has had several students over the years attend UCF, so I picked that. I knew I had to convince Dad first. I wasn't sure he would let me go after, well, you know. But we came to an understanding that I would have to wait until the next application cycle to attend and that I would take classes at the Community College of Philadelphia while waiting. I was okay with that. I went to CCP and took about twenty credits between the summer and the fall sessions, which transferred. In January, we were on a plane to sunny Orlando.

 Anna Picari

My choice of psychology as a major shocked no one, and Kim was thrilled. I mean, she was weirdly excited. But even though I didn't know it at the time, I now know that Kim understood this was a positive reaction to my depression and attempts, and that perhaps I wanted to learn as much as possible and maybe, one day, help others. And she was right. My dissertation is tentatively titled "Familial Drug Addiction and Its Role in Perpetuating Feelings of Shame and Depression in Teenagers." I don't know if I am going to keep that title, but I'm excited that my research is showing a correlation between teenage depression and substance abuse in parents and caregivers. The kids that I'm interviewing are incredibly resilient and open. The stories they have shared and continue to share are testaments to their strengths.

Just then, I get a notification on my phone that my plane will be boarding in five minutes. I push my empty glass toward the end of the bar and see Noah pouring a beer. He looks up at me and raises his finger for me to wait. He whispers something to the other bartender and slips from under the bar, grabs my carry-on luggage, and we walk out of the restaurant together. Noah walks me to the gate and hugs me as I gather with my boarding group. I whisper "I love you" to him, and he says it back.

I turn with a last wave and walk onto the plane, excited to see my Mattie and every one of my crazy crew.

Kim

By the time I get home, I'm wiped out. I only had four sessions, but the last was a two-hour new couple session. Couples are tough because they often come with personal baggage and traumas and need to get all that sorted out before they can heal the cracks in their partnership. This is true of the couple that I met, and I suggested that we do individual sessions prior to moving to couple's therapy. They did not like this because they were both fearful of someone calling "divorce." Because of this, I had them both write a few sentences committing to the full process and that there would be no discussion of divorce until they have at least four sessions together. They acquiesced, and I will be seeing each of them, alone, next week and the following week.

With couples, it's sometimes a final attempt to fix issues that have been going on for years and have finally hit a boiling point. Basically, for some people, coming to couples therapy is the therapeutic version of a "Hail Mary pass." I admire my clients for being brave enough to dig into their lives and their emotions to try to get emotionally whole.

Then another couple pops into my purview as my parents come in through the back door with a tray of eggplant parmesan and a Caesar salad. I was tasked with bringing the wine and fresh bread to the gathering. Mattie and I set the table earlier, being sure to have her spot safely in the middle of the table. Julia came next, with Deven and Clare not far behind.

Rocky hears Shawn's uber-quiet car coming down the driveway long before the rest of us do. And as soon as he barks, we all rush to the front patio. Oliver gets out of the passenger side with a huge smile on his face, followed by Shawn. Oliver immediately walks to Mattie, lifts her high in the air, and brings her down until they are face to face. She wraps her arms around his neck and hugs the hell out of her brother. When he puts her back on the ground, we all take turns hugging Oliver and telling him how wonderful he looks. His light brown hair is even more golden, as if he's had professional highlights. Maybe he has, or maybe it's from the sun, but the light tan that he sports year-round is definitely from the sun. He looks amazing and happy and relaxed.

Once in the house, everyone sits at their seat at the table, which is a long heirloom farm table with benches and upholstered chairs on each end, which are my parents' designated seats. It makes my heart swell with love at the fact that everyone here has claimed their place. Mom and I pour wine for the adults and grape juice for Mattie. I take my seat on the right side of Mattie since Oliver always sits on her left. Shawn is next to me.

Oliver stands and says, "Congratulations, Mattie Angela Orsetti-McDaniel! You are a first grader now! We love you so much." Oliver raises his glass, and we follow suit. Mattie loves being called by her full name.

"Oliver, clink my glass," Mattie demands, and we all laugh and ready ourselves to eat.

Just then, Deven stands, and Clare rises next to him, and it takes a few seconds for us to notice. They grab each other's hands and announce, "We're engaged!"

The cheers are deafening, and Rocky is barking, not sure if he should bark in his happy bark or in his stranger-danger bark. I scramble to my feet and run over to them and hug them together.

I tell them how much I love them and tell Clare that she's now officially one of us and has to put up with all of our insanity. She laughs and agrees and welcomes hugs and congratulations from everyone. Before the evening ends, Mattie has secured her spot as flower girl.

Oliver

I knew that Deven was going to ask Clare to marry him. Clare is the perfect fit for Deven, and I am so happy for the both of them. Deven also knows about Noah. He and Clare have come to Florida, and we have hung out a few times. Deven thinks Noah is good for me, and I totally agree. Noah told me that if the rest of my family are anything like Deven and Clare, he already loves them.

I walk the happy couple to their car after hugging Jules goodbye and watching her drive ridiculously fast down the driveway.

Deven man-hugs me and says, "It's good to see you. How long are you staying?" I tell him that I will be in Pennsylvania for five days, and we set up a time to go out. I hug Clare, and they both wave before getting into their car.

I walk over to the rope swing that hangs from a thick branch of an oak tree and take a seat, pushing myself a little with my right foot. I have a good view of the house and the cottage. I think about everyone who lives here and comes here and belongs here, and my heart is full of gratitude and love. I feel fortunate to be living this crazy life with people who love me unconditionally.

Kim

It's almost 11 p.m. and I just finished emptying the dishwasher. I walk to the den where Shawn is watching an extra innings Phillies game. I kiss him on the top of his head and tell him that I'm heading outside for a few minutes. He doesn't question me because this is sometimes where I go to meditate. I grab an old sweater from my cubby in the laundry area and go out to the back patio, followed by Rocky. It's still warm in Pennsylvania, but I appreciate the pleasant and gentle breeze as I sit back on my favorite outdoor lounge chair. My furry companion snuggles up next to me as I look up at the perfect night sky. It's filled with stars and a moon serving as a night light, and I reflect on the day.

Although Matthew is a beautiful background shadow, he is the impetus for my present life. Through our short time together, he taught me how to appreciate and celebrate life's smaller things (such as my new ritual of celebrating the first day of the school year) and how to truly be alive and to love in this mad world. His DNA surrounds me every day in Julia's spontaneity and in Deven's warmth. It inadvertently runs through Mattie's life because she is bonded with Julia and Deven. His love surrounds me because he taught me what it means to love as I love Shawn and my other son, Oliver. Tears stream down my cheeks as I laugh when I realize that Matthew's life is intertwined with the lives of each member of my crazy and beautiful family.

Acknowledgments

When I first sat down to write, I had no idea what the process entailed, but I did have the love and encouragement from a bunch of people, and the companionship of my dog.

First and foremost, I need to express excessive gratitude to my husband, daughter, and son. They have cheered me on, given me both solicited and unsolicited suggestions, and the space to write. Their unending love and positivity sustain me both personally and professionally.

Thank you to my mom, Angelina. She is the best mom and the template for my mothering. She has always supported anything that I wanted to do. She is the role model for both me and my amazing sister, Julie, as well as her granddaughters and has taught us all to be strong, confident, independent, and capable women—and how to make the perfect gravy (Italian red sauce).

To my alphas: See dedication page. I love you all!

To: Sarah, Sharon, Jessica, Renee, Stefanie, and Kristina: your input was invaluable, your opinions varied, and your sense of humor moved me forward during the times that I wanted to sink into a gallon of Rocky Road. I am thankful for your honesty and input.

Thank you to Karen and Gina for making Kana real. You are extraordinary women, and I am lucky to have you in my life.

A huge thank-you to the talented Lynn Andreozzi for the eye-catching cover design. You made my book look cool, eye-catching, and intertwined!

And last, and by no means least, I need to extend an enormous thank-you to my editor, Nicole Frail, for her support throughout this eighteen-month journey. Her expertise, never-ending patience, and responsiveness made this process so much easier for this first-time author.

Grandpop Vito's Baccalà Salad

Ingredients

Salted cod (dried)
Cold water
1 whole lemon
3 tablespoons olive oil
Salt & black pepper, to taste
Greek pepperoncini
Kalamata olives
Sweet vinegar peppers (seeded and chopped)
Capers

Directions

1. Take a salted cod (dried) and put it in a roasting pan. Fill the pan with cold water, be sure to completely cover the dried cod. Cover with plastic wrap and put it in the refrigerator. (If you are doing this in winter in a cold region, you can put the pan in the garage.)

2. The next day, take the pan out of the refrigerator and empty the water, being careful not to dump out the cod! Fill with fresh water and cover with plastic wrap. Put it back in the fridge.

3. The next day, repeat the above. Most people do this process only twice, but my grandfather did it a third time. I only do it twice.

4. When the cod is reconstituted, put it in a moderately sized pot and cover with cold water. Bring to a boil. Let it cook for about 5 minutes. Be sure to keep an eye on it! You don't want it to become a shredded mess.

5. Drain and place it in a medium-sized bowl. Using a fork, cut the cod gently into bite-sized pieces. Squeeze a whole lemon on it and toss. Then add about 3 tablespoons of olive oil and toss again.

6. Add any or all the following: salt (be careful, the cod was salted), black pepper, Greek pepperoncini, Kalamata olives, seeded and chopped sweet vinegar peppers, capers.

7. Toss again and eat with "good" Italian bread. Mangia!

Mental Health Resources

If you or someone you know is struggling with mental health issues or suicidal ideation or intention, please reach out to one of the organizations listed below:

Emergency Services
- Call 911 if you are in immediate danger or need urgent help.

988 Suicide & Crisis Lifeline
- **Phone:** 988
- **Text:** 988
- **Website:** https://988lifeline.org

National Suicide Prevention Lifeline
- **Phone:** 1-800-273-8255 (TALK)
- **Text:** Text HELLO to 741741 to connect with a crisis counselor.
- **Website:** suicidepreventionlifeline.org

The Trevor Project (LGBTQ+ Youth)
- **Phone:** 1-866-488-7386
- **Text:** Text "START" to 678678
- **Website:** thetrevorproject.org

Crisis Text Line

- **Text:** Text HOME to 741741 to connect with a crisis counselor.
- **Website:** crisistextline.org

SAMHSA's National Helpline

- **Phone:** 1-800-662-HELP (4357)
- **Website:** samhsa.gov/find-help/national-helpline
- Provides confidential and free help from public health agencies to find substance use treatment and information.